**How Hollywood Can Take Back the Internet
and Turn Digital Dimes Into Dollars**

Andrei Jezierski

iUniverse, Inc.
New York   Bloomington

Television Everywhere

iUniverse books may be ordered through booksellers or by contacting:

iUniverse
1663 Liberty Drive
Bloomington, IN 47403
www.iuniverse.com
1-800-Authors (1-800-288-4677)

Because of the dynamic nature of the Internet, any Web addresses or links contained in this book may have changed since publication and may no longer be valid. The views expressed in this work are solely those of the author and do not necessarily reflect the views of the publisher, and the publisher hereby disclaims any responsibility for them.

ISBN: 978-1-4502-6005-3 (dj)
ISBN: 978-1-4502-6004-6 (ebook)

Printed in the United States of America

iUniverse rev. date: 09/24/2010

"We can't afford to turn analog dollars into digital pennies"
Jeffrey Zucker, CEO NBC Universal
on various occasions in 2008

"I think we're at digital dimes now"
Jeff Z.
March 2009

*"I **am** big. It's the pictures that got small"*
Norma Desmond, *Sunset Boulevard*

*"Everything is vague to a degree you do not realize
until you have tried to make it precise"*
Bertrand Russell

For my son Alex, who always wants to fast-forward live television.

Contents

Exhibits

IV. HOLLYWOOD EVERYWHERE

Acknowledgements

E VEN A MODEST monograph like this one couldn't have been written without help and thoughtful contributions from many along the way. In preparing this book I've spoken with several dozen people, some multiple times, both at the center of today's television industry and at newer-generation ventures aspiring to help transform it. To all of you – and you know who you are – thank you.

While the focus of this book is steadfastly television, its underlying and most practical ideas aren't really about TV at all. They're about the economics and benefits of building direct connections between consumers and services with today's new generation of software applications – whether web-based, browser-accessed services like Google Docs, or light, easy-to-use functionality as in iPhone "apps."

So, whatever benefit and utility you may find here should also be credited to my resolutely non-TV watching colleague Michael Spencer, whose lucid observations about software and whose talent for concise analysis helped shape what this book is about, or at least the good bits.

Additionally I'd like to thank: Ed Simnett for his views on the mobile internet and the larger problem of personalizing internet usage of which "Television Everywhere" is only a special case; Marty Hyman for his always-useful perspectives on service provider economics; Prof. Barry Nalebuff of the Yale School of Management for frameworks with which to improve strategic thinking, especially in a complex and interdependent network of multi-industry participants; Bill Abrams for his insights and practical thoughts on digital rights and current television deals.

On a more personal note, very special thanks to my private television focus group and research panel: Kelley McShane and Jessica McShane. Thanks to Tess Mackin for keeping me elegantly caffeinated, reawakening my appreciation of art and creativity and my respect for people who make beautiful things, all in the midst of writing's daily grind. Thanks also to Tom Reindel whose friendship, business insights, and personal example have helped sustain me for nearly twenty years.

Finally, to a beautiful person without whose unwavering support, grace, steadfast friendship, and unconditional love this would not have been possible: Michelle Genovesi. Thank you.

Introduction: Television Everywhere

"**T**ELEVISION EVERYWHERE" IS on the way. It's a generic term for using the internet to get TV to more devices in more places more conveniently – what you want, where you want, when you want it. It's far from a new idea. Plenty of futuristic notions of TV have been promoted in the past, usually by technologists with a shaky understanding of the television business.

But this time Hollywood's content ownership combined with new, simple technologies could enable the television industry itself to take the lead and modernize television, while extending its economic life well into the future.

More important than delivering TV through the internet is using the internet to retain and expand audiences for the TV we already have. That's what this book is about, and it offers a few practical ideas to people in and around the industry on how to do it.

Since before the internet, sweeping visions (convergence! interactive!) of new devices and video networks have held out the promise of additional convenience for viewers and of new revenue opportunities for content owners and advertisers. Yet for nearly two decades, Television of the Future utopias – featuring over-reaching, not ready for prime-time technologies, abstract futurism, and large investment banking fees – have failed to get on the air. These episodic fevers ranged from the Time-Warner "Full Service Network", to the aborted Bell Atlantic/TCI merger, to Americast, to Tele-TV, to the AOL/Time-Warner epic mega disaster, to the Telcos' boringly familiar warmed-over cable service.

Meanwhile, the world of actual television barely noticed. Today, US viewers spend record amounts of time watching plain old "linear" TV, time-shift a bit of it, and use around 1% of that time to watch video via the internet.

Television's greatest challenge isn't (yet) the internet upending the industry but rather that, apart from Nielsen top 10 programming, both watching and supplying TV in a 400-channel universe have become too complex.

If you're a viewer, it's too hard to discover, locate and organize what you like to watch. If you're a supplier, it's too hard, too hit-or-miss, and too expensive to find, attract and retain audiences, and the window in which to do so continues to shrink.

Programs disappear unknown, unsampled, unwatched, into a zombie world of brand and channel clutter, schedule confusion, and unreached audiences, just like the advertising that pays for them. This waste is the outcome of shopworn marketing methods and winner-take-all business models that are poorly adapted to the distribution complexity and audience fragmentation we already have, never mind the digital arrival of Hulu, Netflix, Amazon, and iTunes.

For Hollywood, it's not the internet per se that's unwelcome. Big Media continues to own and control the content no matter where it's distributed, and in Comcast/NBCU's case they'd literally own a chunk of the internet as well. What's unwelcome is the erosion of television's unique value proposition: mass audience reach.

Instead of being feared as an instrument that takes television audiences apart, the internet can be used to keep them together, sustaining the core of TV's scale-based economic model. The very internet accused of conspiring to turn analog dollars into digital pennies can be pressed into service to blunt the economic effects of TV's self-inflicted fragmentation.

Over the last five years or so, the internet evolved to include software technologies which make it possible to do a broad range of new things cheaply, quickly, experimentally, and adaptably, but at serious scale as well. Gone is much of the need for Big Bang, Grand Projects and huge up-front I.T. infrastructure investments to support them. Nicholas Carr's once controversial assertion, "IT Doesn't Matter", has become a near truism. Or as Ethernet inventor Bob Metcalfe wryly observed, "Carr's [*Harvard Business Review*] article just won't stay debunked."

Inexpensive scalable infrastructure, bite-sized (often browser-based) "apps" and the marketplaces that distribute them have transformed the economics of building and distributing consumer software. This software evolution has simultaneously fueled and benefited from a parallel improvement in the simplicity and usability of consumer devices (the exemplar being the iPhone, iPod Touch, iPad family).

The new software and device technologies, the social processes (often open source) for their development, and the marketplace models for their distribution have democratized who can have an on-going, active connection with a consumer. Not ethereal "brand conversations" existing only in the minds of "digital strategists", but actual connections to end users in the same sense as high-traffic websites or frequently-used iPhone apps. And, to co-opt a bit of marketing babble, surely few categories are as "high involvement" or "engaged" with consumers as media itself? Television has long been a medium waiting to take the next step, to more (inter)actively connect with its audience. In that respect, television and the new software and device technologies are ready-made for each other.

By 2020, it's conceivable that as much as a quarter of TV-watching could shift from being linear and passive (plop down on the couch, grab the remote, what's on TV/the DVR?) to being more like using an application. For example: pull out the iPhone, check the 'myTV' playlist, pick a preview clip you tagged earlier, select the corresponding full episode, point the iPhone at the television, an on it goes.

Much of the physical behavior (couch, device in hand, look at the living room TV, etc.) might be identical. Indeed such familiarity would be a good thing, easing viewers' transition to doing things differently in a "digital" world in ways that the VCR and, to a lesser but still disappointing degree, the DVR failed to do in the analog one. But the convenience, intelligence, program selection criteria, and even the sources of the "programs" themselves will become noticeably different.

Many will be trying their hand at realizing at least some of Television Everywhere's intent, i.e. viewer convenience and content ubiquity. Roughly, these efforts so far are of two sorts, from a very familiar losing playbook: (1) new boxes (though mainly software), and (2) complex networks of vertically-integrated infrastructure and services.

New boxes: Direct-to-consumer media "god boxes" and gadgets come in waves, often venture-backed (hence the fads, er, waves) and are, as a rule, doomed for two major reasons. The primary reason is that cable and/or satellite companies still call the shots on what set top boxes go into the home, despite the emergence of some marginally and grudgingly "open" technical standards. The other reason is that all too often the well-intentioned, ambitiously innovative boxes are complex, stand-alone inventions rather than intuitive appliances, and have poor connections to the surrounding world of services and other devices.

The rare exception to this problem has been the TiVo/DirecTV DVR. Though TiVo remains a financial failure, it became the benchmark of what a DVR should be. The new boxes category is important as a source of ideas and technical innovation, despite a long history of coming and going with barely a trace of market impact.

Complex networks: The other losing play is the deployment of complex, vertically-integrated (and, by the way, largely closed despite protestations to the contrary) service networks. They come from the usual suspects in the usual form: dubiously grand projects of the type envisioned by the Time-Warners or Comcasts, or even BBCs ("Project Canvas") complete with many of the familiar warnings signs.

Once again we are back in the world of utopian "universal platforms," yet more complex authentication and digital rights management schemes, and so forth. Each signature technical issue is more than enough to deep-six an entire project, never mind the awkward matter of new content distribution rights or, even more fundamentally, just what a viewer is to make of all this.

And just what content will be these systems deliver "Everywhere"? That's far from clear. The US cable industry appears to be accidentally/on-purpose misconstruing channel participation in modest "TV Everywhere" technical trials as something more than that. As though when a channel joins a technical experiment it means they'll later simply give away internet-related content rights as part of existing carriage or retransmission fees in a real deployment. That will most assuredly not be the case.

As an analogy, recall the not long-ago handwringing about "the mobile internet?" What would it be? Did we have to build a brand new internet? How would "users" "interact" with it? What about mobile advertising? Should everyone have a .mobi website in addition to their regular one? Etc., etc., etc. Pretty soon the problem went away – Google got better at mobile rendering (i.e. adapting web content for mobile display), the iPhone came along with a browser that wiped out most of the differences between "mobile" and not, and the mobile internet went back to being, well, just the internet.

What the cable guys are doing – that's the TV version of "the mobile internet."

Instead of Television Everywhere's playbook of the past (new boxes/complex networks), today's simplified internet technologies offer a faster, more direct and much less risky route to modernizing what it means to watch (and distribute) TV. In the right hands, these tools could be used to extend the economic viability of linear TV, forge a more direct relationship between content suppliers and viewers, and in doing so prepare for the day down the road when television and the internet really do become one.

Hollywood itself is best placed to define and lead a third, different approach to Television Everywhere. This book is about how to do that.

As much as possible, we've tried to confine ourselves to specific, practical ideas. There are, however, three broad themes which help organize the book and undergird its point of view:

(1) *People like TV.* So much utter nonsense has been put forth about television dying – and its corollary: the internet is doing the killing – that we felt obliged to put together a section debunking this with facts.

Traditional television, despite its problems, is strong and can be made stronger still. Minimizing televisions' strength – which at bottom is as simple as people like to watch TV – and exaggerating the timing and nature of the digital threat, lead to bad decisions about the industry's future business model.

If you're in television or advertising the data we present will likely be familiar, though skimming a few of the quantitative charts wouldn't hurt, especially to share with your digital friends. If you're, say, a software industry person unfamiliar with the territory, then what we offer can bring you quickly up to speed on the basics.

(2) *If you help them, they will stay.* The television industry can start using the internet right now to build a virtuous cycle which modernizes linear TV, keeps people watching it, all the while positioning Hollywood at the head of the line for future digital profits. We elaborate on this idea by defining in detail what we mean by 'help', 'them', and 'watch'.

We define a six-part framework for what 'help' means (from discovering shows, to rewarding viewers for watching them), and how to treat television viewing more like a software-based application which younger viewers especially are accustomed to, and less like a passive, linear activity. We look at segmenting viewers ('them') and how helping is likely to vary by viewer segment. Finally, we look at how to optimize the economics of 'watch'ing and paving the way towards digital viewership.

(3) *Be quick, keep it simple.* Hollywood's window of opportunity is now because:

- the industry is in a position of strength: it maintains firm control over content rights, and linear TV today is healthy, not in crisis

- it has already built popular, branded "starter assets" on the internet, most notably via the Hulu consortium, but also by network, channel, or show

- with today's streamlined internet technologies and infrastructure, especially for consumer applications, simple trumps complicated, small incremental improvements trump endlessly-awaited big bang projects. From a standing start, Hollywood has a good shot at bypassing and outperforming the usual suspects (e.g. cable operators, media gadget promoters) and their likely failure-prone projects.

- either as partners, competitors, or both, expect to hear quite a bit from Google and Apple. So, strategically it's important that Hollywood position itself as something more than "just a library", building leverage for what is likely to be a future digital shoving match.

It's time to get beyond the idea that it's either/or, that it's analog dollars vs. digital pennies, that television and the internet are inherently paired in a race to the bottom.

In the decade or more transition period ahead, old-fashioned television and the internet can be good for each other. "Good" meaning consumers can have greater choice and control over what they watch, while television's unique value proposition of mass reach advertising is preserved. "Good" meaning internet-based television can reinforce program and even channel brands rather than weakening them. And "good" meaning the combined revenues of internet- and traditionally-distributed programming can grow rather than flatten or decline.

It's quite likely the internet will eventually turn television into a different medium altogether. Not only can Hollywood strongly influence the pace and outcome of that transformation, it's in the television industry's vital interest that it begin acting to do so right now, not wait for that reality to be defined by others.

In the early 1950s, Pat Weaver was architect of both NBC's break-through programming innovations and the genius behind the revolution in television broadcasting's business model which survives to this day. He was on the scene as the industry wrestled with the threat of a transformational shift of profits from radio to TV. In his memoirs he described it this way:

"Though NBC Television was now operating at a profit, the revenue wasn't even remotely sufficient to carry the entire network. We were sharply aware of the danger that radio might die before television became big enough to replace it...

"We stressed the fact that radio and television were complementary media. They needed each other. You could advertise on a TV hit that millions of radio listeners would never see. To reach a complete audience, you had to advertise on both."

We don't subscribe to "death of television" pseudo-futurism. Today's broadcast television is not 1950s radio (a medium, by the way, that adapted and continues to do well). Nor is today's internet video (yet) analogous to the explosively growing broadcast TV business of that bygone era. As we'll see in the course of this book, however, Weaver's strategic thinking and his cautionary and prescient insights about the transformational shift in business profitability are highly relevant to the television industry challenges ahead.

Parodied in its very own products as chaotic, arbitrary-seeming, and deal-obsessed, Hollywood also has a long history of adaptability, resourcefulness and, most of all, survival. Let's hope that despite the industry's concentration into huge corporate conglomerates those qualities still endure. If Hollywood steps in to organize what the internet has already unleashed – increased consumer choice and cheaper distribution technology – it once again has a generational opportunity to reshape the media industry in its favor, preserving and possibly expanding its role just as it did with the advent of television itself over sixty years ago.

I. How We Got Here

The Future Foretold

ENTERING THE LOBBY of AOL's Virginia headquarters, we saw Rahm Emanuel exit briskly toward the black town car idling at the curb. It was late 1999, and this was the first of two glimpses of TV's future which we stumbled upon that day.

Emanuel had recently left the Clinton West Wing and set up shop at Wasserstein Perella & Co., an investment banking boutique. Shortly after our sighting, Wasserstein was identified as one of the principal advisers in the epic Time-Warner AOL deal. Sold to shareholders as catapulting the old media of movies, television, cable, and magazines into AOL's internet age, the $180 billion deal became the signature, synergy-filled, shareholder-value destroying, mega-disaster of the dotcom bubble.

The second, larger revelation of the day was mounted on the lobby's blond wood paneling – AOL's mission statement: *"To build a global medium as central to people's lives as the telephone or television... and even more valuable."*

A new medium, maybe not AOL's alone... but like television, … everywhere.

Ten years later everyone including Rahm Emanuel had long moved on. Little in the intervening decade worked out according to the prevailing grand visions. The dotcom and telecom bubbles imploded. The media deal of the century was an outright failure, accomplishing little more than a bit of cross-property advertising with dubious transfer prices. Once the king of the consumer internet, AOL and its wildly-spinning management turnstile rode the decline of dial-up internet service into obscurity. Finally, AOL was unceremoniously kicked to the curb by Time-Warner CEO Jeff Bewkes and sent on its way.

The internet, not AOL, became the global medium "as central to people's lives as the telephone and television." So global a medium in fact, both in scale and scope, that it is absorbing the telephone and, experts say, setting to work next on television.

Television Everywhere

Television Everywhere isn't a new idea. It's been around since before there was an Everywhere. It's the latest name for the latest version of an attempt to transform the medium. In theory, it's about using the internet to help bring viewers what they want, when they want, where they want it – any program, any time, any device.

Before there was a commercial internet there was the idea of combining assorted home activities with TV watching, paving the path to... well, the future. Video on demand. Shopping. Electronic mail. Video conferencing.

Describing the Time-Warner Full Service Network for its readers in 1994, The *New York Times* noted: "Viewers will turn on their television sets to see a rotating carousel on the screen that will allow them to select and watch specific movies at any time of day" (note to *Mad Men* fans – not a wheel, but a "carousel"). The article went on to cite the Time-Warner venture as but one of "more than 30 significant trials."

Over the last decade or more two sorts of activities have been justified to shareholders and regulators as strategic, transformational moves aimed at turning television into something bigger: Deal-making at the top, technology from the bottom.

Let's start with technology. Across the consumer landscape there's a long history of technology posing as a solution, on a quest to find a problem. Most of the time that fails, but every once in a while you get a TiVo, or a Blackberry, or an iPod/iTunes, or an iPhone. Something which both changes the game and makes a lot of money (for TiVo, not so much). Like Hollywood itself, most technology entrepreneurs understand and accept this long-odds, home-run way of doing business. Cable companies, and certainly phone companies, don't.

The temptation for network operators (i.e. cable, telcos), however, has been irresistible. From the decade-and-a-half old example of the Full Service Network, to telcos' new and economically-doomed mobile TV, carriers still cannot stop conjuring for themselves images of new, big monthly subscription fees, slices of all sorts of consumer transactions, dancing like sugar plum fairies in Christmas dreams.

And so, yet another set of network experiments. Wireless cable service, for example, was one of the last fads – BellSouth Entertainment and whatnot (Surely, not even Disney imagineers would think of juxtaposing the words "Bell" and "entertainment"?). In fairness to the phone companies' intelligence there was also a hidden agenda especially when newer, fiber optic networks were involved: muddle the costs of TV and other new Jetson-like networks with those of regulated businesses. Thus capital expenditures for rolling out fiber would be subsidized by rate payers, and the infrastructure they helped pay for would enable unregulated (i.e. uncapped) revenues from futuristic new services.

Today, telcos have simply given up on TV of the future and have been busily rolling out Television of the Past – boring imitations of cable TV. In any event, the remnants of and successors to the "more than thirty significant trials" sank into the quicksand, sometimes hastened by the pile driver of "moving up the value chain" – consulting babble for phone companies trying (well, vaguely aspiring) to do what Hollywood does. There was even, for a mercifully brief time, a Bell Atlantic Studios. Seriously.

Which brings us back to the first of the two approaches to television industry makeovers: deal-making at the top. In the last decade, media investment bankers were the arms merchants of the "Content is King" wars in which media tycoons alternately integrated content (movies, television production) and some distribution (broadcast station groups, cable channels, DVD sell-through), and then promptly ripped them apart again.

At one level, one might argue there was a strategic rationale, or at least concern – (further) integrate content as a defensive move against distributors (i.e. cable and telcos consolidating their power, as well as reinforcing the moat against whatever that internet thing might do. If we control all of content and some distribution (broadcast, maybe satellite), went the thinking, then, well, we're in control. And by the way, why should US media forgo the obvious economic and regulatory benefits of industry concentration and cartelization like, well, every other industry from financial services, to healthcare, to telecom, to energy, to agribusiness, etc.?

At another level, this period resembled not much more than a poker game in which a few guys named Murdoch, Malone, Diller, Turner, Redstone, Levin, Eisner, etc., went back and forth while shareholders looked on, hoping the player they'd staked would emerge the winner.

Time-Warner/AOL was the largest hand ever played – the watershed deal in both the quest for bigness and the obviousness of failure. From that "peak", the massive multi-decade US consolidation of movies, television, newspapers, magazines, cable and satellite into Big Media exhausted itself, soon to be followed by sporadic unwindings.

Viacom and CBS separated. After years of pursuit, no sooner had it successfully captured DirecTV as the jewel in its global satellite crown, News Corp. traded it away in a complex, vintage Malone/Murdoch deal. IAC Interactive was in a perpetual state of becoming. Time-Warner itself implicitly acknowledged failure by changing their ticker symbol from the embarrassing 'AOL' back to the old 'TWX'. They have since divested their music division, spun out their cable business, and unceremoniously shed what was left of AOL. And at the rate the magazine business is going, they might even separate Time from Warners.

Meanwhile, a company named "Google", founded a year before the Time-Warner AOL deal was announced, built a stream of advertising revenue that came to exceed that of ABC, CBS, and NBC combined, and made what seemed an ominously threatening deal of its own – it bought YouTube.

Television Reality

We've recounted in very broad strokes the flavor of what, for the last decade or more, occupied and pre-occupied companies that make media, distribute it, or aspired to. Like corporate America generally but only more so, Hollywood's executive suite shares a love of Big Moves. And given the industry that it is, that love easily becomes a self-perpetuating obsession intensified by the Sun Valley, *Vanity Fair*, mogul/proprietor ethos that often prevails. How else to explain tragedies like Ted Turner's self-marginalization or (sorry, but one last mention) the AOL/Time-Warner fiasco itself.

As for TV of the Future, seemingly dozens of at least aspirational (keywords: "convergence", "interactive"), if not operational, efforts to bring together the internet, computers, and television together did not. Also cancelled were the wild (and wildly vague) visions of telcos and internet service providers squeezing into the media club – phone guys somehow power lunching as Hollywood equals at The Ivy.

This has all been previously recounted of course, and much more interestingly, colorfully, and at great length by industry observers like Ken Auletta or Michael Wolff. We tailgate on the Big Moves issue (deals, silver-bullet technology) here for two reasons.

First, taking the long view, Hollywood has a history of resourceful deal-doing that actually makes a difference, it just hasn't been much in evidence recently. We believe that culture and those capabilities, while dormant and/or misused of late, are still there and will turn out to be important once again, down the road. To refresh your memory and try to strengthen that historical case, we'll do a quick recap of Hollywood's television age momentarily.

Secondly, by noting Big Moves' inherent limitations in creating value either for customers or shareholders, we clear the way to changing the subject to things that are much more practical, can be done right now, and don't necessarily require the sanction of the "CEO agenda." So, instead we discuss an alternative agenda – adapting televisions' day-to-day business to the changing reality of what viewers want first, and putting deal-doing second. The saddest and most telling flaw in all the Big Move talk is that the words "customer" or "viewer" or "audience" or "advertiser" are used in only the most cursory, pro forma, jargon-filled sort of way. If at all. At the end of the day, ideas that don't focus on those constituencies won't create value, a fatal omission that could help clear the way for the likes of an Apple or a Google to meet their needs instead.

Let's wrap up this chronology of the last decade or so on a positive note which we'll look at in more up-to-date detail in the following chapter – the strength of the television industry. It was a very good decade for both the real television industry, and for the internet infrastructure that is allegedly going to be the instrument of television's death.

In television, the industry's total advertising revenues grew over 40%, average US television viewing per person increased by around 17%, and prime-time broadcast CPMs nearly doubled. Oh, and despite the metastasis of the "reality" genre, HBO aired *The Sopranos* and some other good stuff, and *Mad Men* came along.

Broadband penetration, even in the laggard US, crossed well past the 50% mark, finally making access to video over the internet reasonably commonplace. Wireless carriers transitioned to data-friendlier 3G networks. Apple launched the iPhone. Subscriptions to wireless data plans rapidly accelerated, with the iPhone device family accounting for half of US mobile internet traffic by the first quarter of 2009.

Thanks to the internet, consumers have more control than ever over their media choices – just ask newspaper and magazine publishers. In print media, the internet has begun the fundamental change of moving the distribution model away from physical media, but also away from editorial and brand loyalty, away from subscription revenues, and towards much more consumer choice, greater audience fragmentation, and (from the consumer's point of view) cheap or free.

Television is far from being under similar assault yet, much less dead, and enjoys much greater uniqueness of and control over its content than print media. Hence TV has a much longer runway with which to deal with the internet's strategic challenge. Nevertheless, the medium will assuredly change. And taking the long view, Hollywood has proven itself more than capable at adapting to tectonic shifts and *Survivor*-like experiences, coming out stronger than ever.

Let's take a quick look at just how strong and effective Hollywood's ability to adapt has been, starting with its first major death threat – television itself.

Plywood Boxes

We've seen this movie before. Sixty years ago Hollywood was marked for death. "Television" had arrived and it was free, convenient, modern and soon insinuated itself into the very fabric of the post-war consumer lifestyle. But instead of dying, the studios overcame adversity much like the resourceful heroes in their own movies. They transformed, recombined, and survived an often chaotic, sometimes near-death ride to prosperity, re-emerging at the center of a much-consolidated entertainment industry.

Jack Gould, *The New York Times'* newly minted television critic wrote in 1947:

> *"Up to now the Hollywood film industry has carried on a cautious flirtation with television – trying to decide whether it should woo the girl and bring her into the family or hit her on the head with the big financial rolling pin it possesses."*

In 1946, Twentieth Century Fox's Darryl Zanuck is said to have remarked: "Video [meaning television] won't be able to hold onto any market it captures after the first six months. People will soon get tired of staring at a plywood box every night." As time went on, other studios weren't quite so sanguine – former Disney CEO Michael Eisner recalls that as a child, the RKO theater marquee in his neighborhood admonished, "Don't watch TV."

But of course people did. By 1952, The *Times'* Gould wrote of "a medium which in six years has grown from a novelty to a habit for 50,000,000 people." By 1956, 65% of US households had televisions (up from less than 5% when Zanuck spoke ten years earlier) and watched them for about 5 hours per day.

The year 1946 turned out in many ways to be a high water mark for the movie business. Theatrical film admissions hit an all-time high of 4.1 billion for the year, the post-war economic boom was underway, and the threat of television was still over the horizon. Hollywood's vertically-integrated business model was still intact, although the Justice Department had restarted the war-delayed anti-trust process aimed at what they called "divorcement" of exhibitors from film studios.

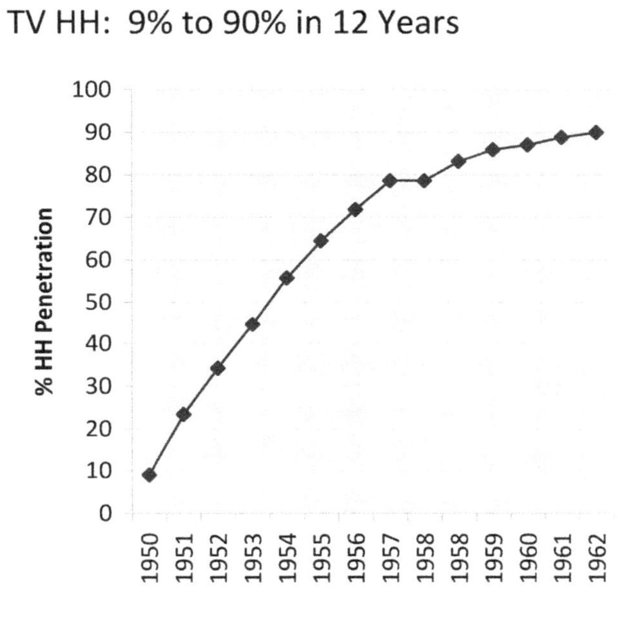

TV HH: 9% to 90% in 12 Years

Exhibit I-1: US television households 1950-1962

When television first emerged, it was a business completely apart from movies. "Plywood box" manufacturers themselves, such as RCA, often owned and controlled the growing networks of broadcast stations. The early programming business model was to sell off entire slots of airtime in fifteen-, thirty-minute, or hour-long units to individual sponsors who, helped by the broadcasters and advertising agencies, developed their own programs. Early, experimental prices for television time were set in reference to what national radio shows could command, but rapidly became more expensive as television audiences mushroomed.

In fact, early television rapidly threatened to become a victim of its own success. A 1941 pilot of NBC's *Truth or Consequences* was priced at $120 for an hour of evening prime time. By 1948, a comparable hour sold for around $11,000, by 1951 it was $35,000, by 1956 almost $70,000. By 1954, television broadcaster revenues had gone from negligible to overtaking all of radio, in little more than a decade.

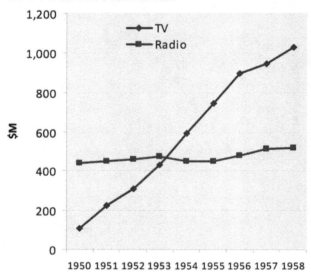

Exhibit I-2: TV vs. Radio Broadcaster Revenues 1950-1958]

The combination of ever-escalating programming costs (higher production values, more expensive talent, etc.), increased audience expectations, and advertisers' rush to the new medium, all rapidly drove up the price of television airtime. This meant fewer national advertisers could afford the single-sponsor programming model. More ominously for the still-emerging TV business, the more dependent broadcasters became on a small handful of big-spending sponsors, the more the entire programming and broadcasting business model could be controlled by a few powerful advertisers, not the new industry itself.

The Google of its day, in the sense of innovating the industry model for advertising in the new medium, was the National Broadcasting Corporation, partial predecessor of today's NBC Universal unit at General Electric. NBC, more specifically vice-president of television programming Pat Weaver (Sigourney Weaver's father, by the way), figured out as early as 1949 how to break the logjam by replacing full sponsorships with alternate arrangements by which companies shared costs from week to week. For example, Philco and Goodyear shared Sunday nights between 1951 and 1955.

From there – and this was the strategic insight – he moved to what he called "participative advertising" in a "magazine format." This is the structure we know today in which broadcasters or independent producers offer up programming into which a broad array of advertisers insert short commercials. This new structure had several important advantages: it further enlarged an already-growing market by enabling many more sponsors to bid for more affordable slices of advertising, and it shifted the balance of power away from single sponsors and ad agencies back to the broadcaster.

Speaking of this revolution in what today would be called a "business model" (as well as the creative revolution in television he sparked with such shows as *Today*, and *Tonight* which still anchor NBC line-ups sixty years later), Weaver wrote in his memoirs:

> *"I joined NBC as head of television [from ad agency Y&R] with an unspoken determination to change the existing system – unspoken, because I didn't dare make too public an issue of it. What I had in mind was a real revolution in broadcasting. And during my years at NBC, I actually managed to carry it off. At first, a lot of people disapproved of what I was doing, especially my former colleagues at the ad agencies. But very soon, as the cost of television sponsorship rose, most of them realized that there were advantages in the new system, especially for the smaller advertisers, who couldn't afford to sponsor an entire program.*

"By the time I left NBC, it owned most of the shows it put on the air, and the other networks had begun to follow. I was proud of that…"

The Weaver revolution effectively brought the curtain down on ad agency programming and its ownership, shifted control to the broadcast network itself, and created a much larger television advertising marketplace. The shift is in many ways analogous to what Google accomplished in internet advertising. Google broke the prevailing AOL- and Yahoo!-style link between portal and search, creating a brand-new ad category that eclipsed display advertising. Search-based advertising expanded the market by creating nearly infinite ad "inventory" at variable, auction-based prices affordable to many small- and medium-sized businesses.

From Vaudeo to Syndication

"Vaudeo" is what industry trade publication Variety dubbed the early days of television. Lacking original programming of its own, television first started by simulcasting vaudeville radio shows and then simply stealing performers from radio. Bob Hope joked, "When vaudeville died, television was the box they put it in."

TV took off in part because it so successfully adapted winning formulas from film and radio, combining movies' excitement with radio's convenience and in-home intimacy. Marshall McLuhan observed that "the content of any medium is always another medium," and that in its early days a new medium tends to copy the content and forms of a prior one.

And so it was with TV. As television grew, it copied programming genres from both movies and radio, and adapted highbrow fare from plays and literature. As a business, it enabled advertisers to reach large-scale national audiences through a genuinely new medium of unprecedented persuasive power.

By the mid-1950s it was glaringly obvious that TV was

substantially shrinking box office receipts. Despite a few skirmishes – marketing wars touting the superiority of the theater experience, or introducing short-lived wide-screen products such as Cinemascope – Hollywood began adapting to the reality of the television age.

US Theatrical Film Admissions

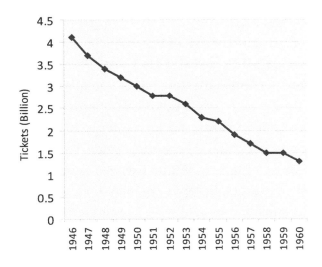

Exhibit I-3: US Theatrical Film Admissions 1946-1960]

Soon, studio infrastructure was used to produce as many hours of television programming as theatrical films. In 1953, Hollywood's nineteen International Alliance of Theatrical Stage Employees locals reported "reasonably full employment" mainly because 25 percent of studio craft workers were engaged in television-related production. In an otherwise down year for movie production, "telefilms", as filmed-entertainment for TV was called, used seven independent lots entirely occupied by television crews.

Film libraries were licensed for television exhibition (Famously, *The Wizard of Oz* was the first feature film to be broadcast on US prime time television in 1956). And, in the ultimate if you can't beat 'em join 'em move, studios produced their own hour-long marquee showcases for prime time television, including *MGM Parade, Warner Brothers Presents,* and *Twentieth-Century Fox Hour*. Also by mid-decade, studios relaxed contractual rules preventing film stars from appearing on television. Among the first to cross over were Charleton Heston, Gene Autry, and Groucho Marx hosting his own show, NBC's *You Bet Your Life*.

The 1950s and much of the 1960s were a creatively fertile time for film, but studios could not stem the financial effects of television's ascent. The so-called Paramount Decree of 1948, which had forced studios to sell off captive theater chains, began to be felt in earnest. Stripped of theater cash flow, studios had a harder time getting bank financing for their pictures and increasingly took on higher risks with higher cost of capital. The studio system itself was crumbling as stars became free agents, studio executives departed to become independent producers, libraries were sold off, and the emergence of television subsidiaries (such as Columbia's Screen Gems, for example) further fragmented the business.

Increasingly distressed, studios rode two waves to become the combined film and television powerhouses that define Hollywood today. The first was a popular business and stock market fad of the so-called "Go-Go Years" in the mid-to-late 1960s: conglomerates. Having a hard time as stand-alone businesses, studios became a glamorous target for acquisitive conglomerateurs. Paramount, for example, was acquired by Gulf + Western Industries in 1966. Despite being bought and sold and generally kicked around, studios were on the whole a bit better cushioned from financial turmoil.

Trustbusters

The second wave was political and regulatory. Old Hollywood's anti-trust saga concluded with the 1948 Paramount Decree stripping them of their theater chains, but television's was just about to begin.

In 1970, TV networks were hit with the Financial Interest and Syndication rules, or Fin-Syn.

Essentially an anti-trust measure prohibiting vertical integration of production and distribution, Fin-Syn barred broadcast networks from participating financially in the syndication (i.e. rerun) business. Cut off from the syndication profit stream, high production costs couldn't be recouped, so broadcasts networks outsourced a good deal of production to Hollywood studios, now eager to step in and further fill the gap. Even by itself, the new steady diet of television production business created by the legal separation helped rejuvenate Hollywood. On top of that, enabling studios rather than broadcasters to have a stake in the increasingly (often hugely) profitable annuity streams from program syndication gave Hollywood a golden goose.

Finally, in the early 1990s Fin-Syn itself was swept away in the prevailing tide of deregulation. The conditions to create today's Big Media oligopolies took shape as the barriers to combining television distribution and Hollywood were removed, and more cash was infused into the industry.

Hollywood always had an eye for deep-pocketed sugar daddies, be it Howard Hughes, or the late-60's corporate conglomerates. Studios' perennial balance sheet crises, solved temporarily by opportunistic conglomerations such as Gulf + Western buying Paramount or Coca-Cola buying Columbia pictures, predictably ended up both bewildering the new owners and taxing their patience.

By the late 1980s it was Japan, Inc.'s turn. Already buying up all manner of US assets, from Rockefeller Center, to the Pebble Beach golf resort, they were attracted to Hollywood by imaginary synergies between consumer electronics and making movies and TV shows. Truckloads of cash arrived courtesy of Matsushita and Sony.

Having removed barriers to vertical integration, and with financial health now reasonably good for even the weaker players, media promptly set about getting Bigger. News Corp., still a fairly new owner of Twentieth-Century Fox, launched the Fox television network. Disney acquired the ABC television network, Viacom (containing Paramount studios) acquired its former parent, CBS (and later split up again). Sony's arrival brought an array of film and television brands under one roof, and bringing up the rear, industrial conglomerate General Electric combined its NBC television unit with Vivendi's Universal studios.

The combination of refreshed balance sheets and return to vertical integration's multiple revenue streams completed the industry's sixty-year roller coaster ride back to pre-eminence. Fin-Syn first rejuvenated Hollywood with new profit streams from outsourced television production and access to syndication annuities. Then Fin-Syn's elimination brought old rivals together, cementing the highly-integrated production-through-distribution business model at the heart of today's media conglomerates. Hollywood doubled down and never looked back, driving the global spread of American entertainment culture to near hegemony.

For Your Consideration

One of Hollywood's favorite topics is itself. Movies like Robert Altman's *The Player*, or Paddy Chayefsky's *Network*, or the HBO series *Entourage* paint a humorous picture of often alarming venality, crassness, short-term thinking and indifference to "serious" business practices. Funny, but misleading if you're interested in business strategy.

Television and filmed entertainment in general remain a creative, inherently uncertain, home-run driven business. The industry's swagger arguably matches that of Wall Street. Beneath the distracting glitter, however, under the very shadows of the ego-filled moguls it often satirizes, the industry created thoughtful and extremely capable executives: the late Frank Wells, Frank Biondi,

Tom Freston, Peter Chernin, Robert Daly, and (despite whatever actually took place at Yahoo) Terry Semel, to name a few of the more prominent.

These are the sorts of managers who day in and day out keep the wheels on, who try within the limits they're given to forge a long-term economically-sound agenda, and who understand the fundamentally creative, risky nature of the industry, its products, and its talent.

As Hollywood has matured and become more corporate, it has built management capabilities and executive talent that belie much of its reputation as a personality-driven, irrational industry. It's a fundamentally American industry that observers have wrongly pronounced dead countless times, either because it was deemed creatively lost, becoming culturally irrelevant, or doomed to obsolescence by new innovations. Time and again it responds, whether with *Star Wars* or *Ghandi. Avatar* or *The Hurt Locker. M.A.S.H.* or *The Sopranos* or *Mad Men*. DVDs or Hulu.

Our bet is that for the next sixty years Hollywood will be as resourceful as it has been for the last sixty in defining and shaping whatever is to become of television. So far, it has done quite well albeit against a still-early and highly-exaggerated threat. In 2006, there was an outbreak of near-hysteria (in the media, not so much in Hollywood board rooms) over Google's acquisition of YouTube and its future implications for commercial video content.

Since then, TV's response to digital distribution has been a balance of experimentation, partnership, rights protection, and patience. Hulu has been surprisingly well executed, both as industry consortium and as studio-controlled web portal showcasing popular TV shows. Hollywood has added to its still-modest position on the internet through branded network-, channel- and show-specific sites, as well as selective distribution deals with Netflix, etc. The question for this unstable mix is: what's next?

Let's wrap up this industry retrospective on how we got here with three take-aways that we believe bear directly on Hollywood's role in television's future:

- *King Content:* The deck remains fundamentally stacked in Hollywood's favor. Content owners control distribution rights and therefore can strongly influence, if not outright control, the pace and pricing of new forms of distribution.

- *Deal-Doing:* Cari Beauchamp observed in her *Vanity Fair* article and then book on the subject that Joseph P. Kennedy (yes, that patriarch) in the late 1920s "was the first and only outsider to take Hollywood for a ride." Arguably, that record remains unchanged and is something to keep in mind when contemplating technology-led "disruption" scenarios undermining Hollywood's business model.

- *Technology Threats:* Historically, the grander the technical schemes to change television, the more miserably they've failed. We've seen no reason yet to believe that will change. Unlike its music industry cousins, Hollywood has successfully (if at first grudgingly) adapted to and co-opted the main innovations, from cable, to the VCR, to DVDs, to pay-per-view and video on demand.

With these factors and Hollywood's history of resourcefulness in mind, let's move on to taking a look at where we are now.

II. Where We Are

The "Death" of Television

S O IN THE end television didn't kill movies or the studios that made them. But now, according to some experts, the Four Horsemen of the Apocalypse are back riding not colored horses but the internet, and it's TV's turn to die. In fact according to many it's already dying. Except it's not.

Bob Hoffman, ad agency CEO and maker of Toyota Prius commercials by day, *Ad Contrarian* blogger by night, described the Death of Television about as clearly and unambiguously as possible: "It is a story built on shabby journalism, ad industry buffoonery, and the willful suspension of skepticism on a scale unprecedented during my time in the advertising business."

And just because we're management consultants, let's not avert our gaze from our own industry's buffoonery. A staple of the management consulting business is the Death of..., End of..., Future of... oeuvre with apocalyptic overtones. The intention is to scare (the pitches are often called internally "the burning platform") and motivate clients to meet, maybe even to buy. There's a blizzard of smart talk and charts from which all the victim can usually extrapolate is "Gee, maybe I'd better hire these guys because it's so complicated."

Then the impressive volume or presentation ends with a simultaneously vague but very ominous conclusion. Here's an actual one about television, though it sounds as though it could just as easily be about lawn fertilizer. "At a time of exquisite [sic] change in both demand and supply, immediate action is required." It then goes on to prescribe an agenda of exhortative slogans, including such winners as "harness differentiated skills and competencies," reminiscent of China's "Achieve the Four Modernizations!" in the late 1970's, except the Chinese used clearer English and specified actual goals.

The Most Pervasive Medium. Ever.

Let's take a look at just one chart from the US 2009 Video Consumer Mapping Study (yes, funded by partly by Nielsen). Live television has 94% reach for over 300 minutes per day. No other medium on that chart is remotely close. And television penetration measured by HUT (households using television), continues to vastly outstrip broadband internet and substantially exceeds mobile device penetration, especially when counting devices with more than just rudimentary internet-related capabilities.

Of the "three-screen" time (TV, broadband-connected computer, mobile device), more than 99% is TV viewing, around 98% for the youngest, most technology-engaged. So much for televisions' death, even with the Facebook crowd.

The Power of Television

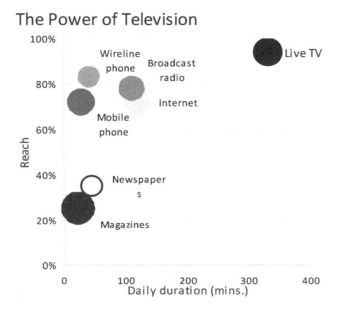

Exhibit II-1: The Power of Television]

Okay, so people may actually *watch* TV, but surely television as a business is rotting from the inside?

Actually, no.

Advertising prices (e.g. primetime CPMs) and total industry ad revenues have grown enormously over the last decade. Despite fluctuations from a general economic downturn and substantial, cyclical variations in media spend from political advertising and special events (Olympics, etc.), revenues remain near all-time highs. And while there is some premature counting of chickens going on regarding a recovery of advertising rates and spending, it's fairly likely that sometime in 2011 the business will have recovered to "normal" levels.

Weekday Prime Time CPMs

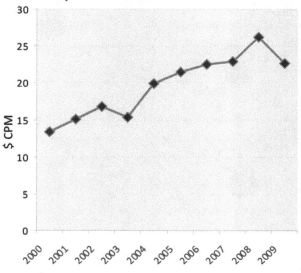

Exhibit II-2: Weekday Primetime CPMs]

US TV Ad Revenues

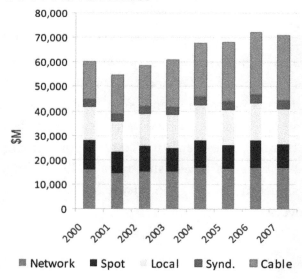

Exhibit II-3: US TV Ad Revenues]

Fragmentation, Not Commoditization

To the extent television has problems, they don't stem from commoditization of content. Outside of largely-marginalized piracy, "the internet" is not a reverse Philosopher's Stone, somehow turning gold into lead, stealing commercial television programming and making it available for free and/or ad free.

Studios are in firm control over how content is windowed (i.e. staged across various forms of distribution: broadcast, syndication, DVD sell-through, etc.), and whether internet-based distribution fits in, if at all. The traditional economics of broadcast, syndication, and ancillary revenues are detailed in the Appendix (*"Hollywood Opts Out of the Google Economy"*) which reprints an analysis (really just a primer) we did years ago when the YouTube-fueled panic first erupted. And, as the title suggested at the time, that business model remains largely unchanged.

Television's "problem" is its own success. In the space of sixty years, we've gone from less than a handful of broadcast channels on air for a few hours per day, to a roughly four-hundred channel universe (counting channel multiplexing and sub-brands, e.g. Discovery, Discovery Kids, Discovery Health, Discovery en Español, etc.) with an enormous number of specialty, enthusiast, and genre cable channels.

While this has been good news for viewers – more stuff, more choices – it's had two complicating effects.

First, total television viewing has been divided over many more channels, thus fragmenting audiences and reducing advertiser reach per channel or program. Fragmented audiences meant chopping advertising spending into a greater number of (smaller) piles. With less money per channel/show to go around: (a) programs have had to get cheaper (one of the main reasons for the proliferation of cheaper-than-scripted, "reality" TV), and (b) media buying has become more complicated – advertising has to be spread over a more complex mix of outlets to meet media buyers' targets for gross ratings points, or other measures of exposure.

Broadcast v. Cable HH Ratings

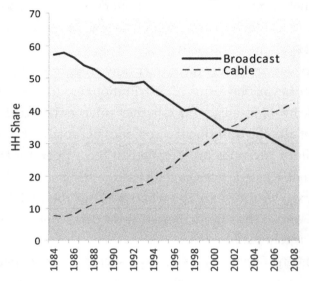

Exhibit II-4: Broadcast vs. Cable HH Ratings]

So what has emerged is a tiered world in which a (very) few channels and programs command (low) double-digit ratings and audience share, but still larger audiences than any other medium can provide. It tails off from there.

The "Audience Tiers" chart shows an audience ratings curve, with highest-rated broadcast and cable channels on the left, and smaller audiences in increasingly niche-focused, specialist channels towards the right. The ratings are for the primetime day part, and live plus same-day (i.e. up to 24-hour DVR delay) viewing for all audiences ("P2+" means persons age two and over) without regard to demographic segmentation. So it's a gross audience measure, averaged over typical primetime ratings. While it's true that an *American Idol*-sized blockbuster hit could have, say, triple the average

Fox prime time ratings, that is far, far from the norm of daily bread-and-butter broadcast network programming.

What's notable is how rapidly and to what level the audiences trail off. We arbitrarily cut the chart into three tiers: over one million, half-a-million to a million, and less than half-a-million. We didn't place all the approximately four hundred channels in the chart, but even in this sampling note the distribution and proportionally how many channels have audiences in the mid-to-high tens of thousands.

Secondly, as the "TV Ad Pricing" chart starkly reminds us, scale or reach is the name of the game in television advertising. Primetime CPMs for thirty-second spots decline sharply as reach declines. So, small audiences combine with low ad prices to produce very low revenues per show. This is moderated only somewhat by the channel's ratings and share "in the demos" (i.e. a more valuable, demographically-based definition of viewership). The combination of the two charts also explains, by the way, why you see enormous quantities of "paid programming"/infomercials during undesirable or near-remnant dayparts on low-rated cable channels. ShamWow!

Connecting the audience tiers to the 'TV Ad Pricing' chart helps you understand that the vast majority of channels combine modest ratings with CPMs well below the rough broadcast network average of around, say, $25. The thin slices on the left of the CPM chart align with the bottom two audience tiers in the audience ratings chart. That matrix is where reality is for most of Hollywood, most shows, and most cable channels. In the end, a channel consistently in the say, mid- or even high-tens of thousands audience size, such as Fuse, or Bloomberg, or Current TV would struggle with profitability, at least on a stand-alone basis, while top-rated networks such as Fox or CBS, or USA or TBS simply print money. There are no "long tail" miracles in the television business, sorry to say.

Audience Tiers

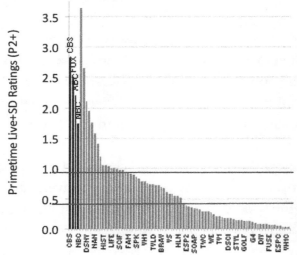

Exhibit II-5: Audience Tiers

TV Ad Pricing: Role of Scale

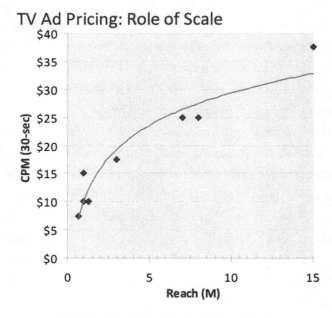

Exhibit II-6: TV Ad Pricing: Role of Scale

Now we turn our attention to what is alleged to be a much more serious threat to linear television than its self-cannibalization – TV over the web.

The Myth of Digital Dimes

Jeff Zucker, CEO of NBC Universal, summarized the conventional view of the internet's threat to TV about as succinctly as possible back in 2008: "We can't replace analog dollars with digital pennies." By March 2009, in part thanks to Hulu's success and NBC's part in it, he'd amended his remarks, replacing "pennies" with "dimes."

But the point remained the same: "digital" would shift audiences, and therefore advertising dollars, from a still-profitable medium to a different one of unknown, but likely much lower future profitability.

So let's look inside the economics of what is sometimes known, a bit pretentiously, as "multiplatform" content. These would be TV shows, distributed through multiple different but somewhat comparable exhibition outlets at the same time, for example: existing linear, plus web-based, plus mobile (if that even turns out to be a different-than-web medium in some significant way).

The digital, multiplatform scenario is different from windowing (i.e. staging various forms of distribution sequentially over time, sometimes with slight overlap. We look at windowing at length in the Appendix). Simultaneous distribution across several different outlets allows each medium to compete for its share of audience using the same content, but addressing distinct viewer technology and lifestyle preferences. For now, at least, the assumption is that each new distribution channel is likely to have substantially different cost and revenue profiles from the tried-and-true Hollywood model of today.

All of this, however, is really just a bunch of prefatory beating around the bush. The fact is that the digital dimes "threat" is a myth and far off one at that. Let's look at three reasons why:

(1) Jeff Zucker himself (and his peers) contained the threat by fiat. Most of their stuff isn't let out of the digital lockbox, so it can't do any threatening. Today's windowing arrangements keep most of what's on TV off the internet. Sure, plenty of clips, highlights, promos, teasers, sometimes a decent archival library, but only a few marquee shows are fully available with, say, twenty-four hour lag (*Daily Show, Colbert Report*, etc.). Today, Hulu or other TV portals plugged into a TV can in no way substitute for a TiVo box with even basic cable or satellite service. And they're not going to be able to for quite a long time.

(2) While small, digital's advertising economics are pretty good. There is every reason to believe in a modest premium for digital CPMs, at least for low-to-mid tier cable fare, in which engagement, attention, and demographic targeting could be superior to linear TV audiences.

(3) To top it off, when you combine (2) above with even the most dire hypothetical shifts to digital viewing, it turns out there isn't a huge gap between the economics of most bread-and-butter linear TV shows and what's likely when you add back in digital distribution (see below). So, in television today any gap between analog and digital is one of dollars to, in a worst-case scenario, somewhat fewer dollars. But then that's not much of a sound bite compared with "digital dimes."

Let's look at these points with some numbers.

First, just how small is "digital"? It's miniscule. The "Monthly Time Spent Viewing" chart shows that even for younger-skewing demographics, internet video delivers (very) low, single-digit percentages of total time spent viewing, and is massively overshadowed by regular old TV. And the single-digit numbers include *all* digital viewing which remains preponderantly YouTube cat videos versus commercial video content. The small online numbers are as true for a popular, but marginally-rated shows like *Gossip Girl,* as they are for mainstream fare like *The Office*

Monthly Time Spent Viewing

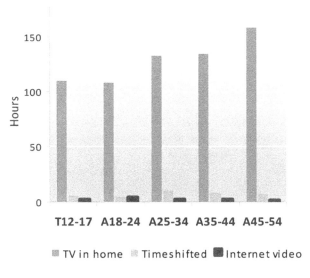

Exhibit II-7: Monthly Time Spent Viewing

Linear vs. Web: Two Popular Examples

Show	Network	P2+ (L+SD)	"Web-equivalent" P2+	Web %	Linear Revs (K)
Gossip Girl	CW	1.02	0.05	4.5	$216
The Office	NBC	8.20	0.03	0.4	$2,400

Exhibit II-8: Linear vs. Web – Popular Examples

Second, digital economics, should they become mainstream, are probably going to be reasonably good. Let's take a look via a hypothetical example. Let's assume that:

- real "cannibalization" would mean a defection of, say, 25% of the linear audience to digital viewing (twenty to fifty times more than today)

- erosion of linear audiences is much more likely in lower-to-mid-tier cable fare which has smaller/more fragmented audiences to begin with

- such an audience is, on average, likely to be more digital-friendly (affinity between geek/"enthusiast" genre shows, for example, and demographics favorable to digital viewing, like skewing young).

Mid-Tier Scenario: (1) Linear Erosion

Rating	P2+ (L+SD)	Broadcast Revenue (K)	25% Shift - Δ Revenue (K)	Net Rev.
1.5	1.7	$620	($78)	(12%)

Exhibit II-9: Scenario – Linear Erosion

So for a hypothetical 1.5 rated mid-tier cable show, dollars don't turn to dimes but as the audience shifts from linear to web-based viewing, we do incur a net loss of about 12% of our revenue mainly due to lower commercial loads (less than half of linear) and a conservative view of web-based CPMs (optimists see them being twice the ad rates for linear TV at comparable scale due to higher "engagement", etc. – we ignored this).

But digital doesn't exist solely as an alternative option to full-episode viewing. Much, possibly most, of the digital viewer activity will be ancillary views of clips, highlights, etc, which surround the show and channel brand whether or not there is any actual defection of linear/analog viewing. So netting out a simple underlying viewing model we developed, in this example we gain back almost all the linear revenue erosion from this modest digital "add-on" phenomenon alone.

Mid-Tier Scenario: (2) Digital $

Digital Viewers (M)	Clips/ Viewer	30-sec Ads/ Clip	CPM	$(K)
0.4	4	1.5	$22.5	$58.2

Exhibit II-10: Scenario – Digital Revenue

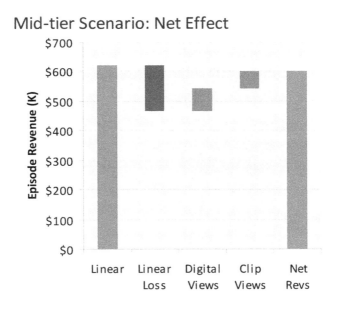

Exhibit II-11: Scenario – Net Effect of Digital Erosion

Finally, to the third point (some shows have more "digital" affinity) – to the extent there are conditions when a meaningful gap exists between the potential economic performance of linear versus digital – what shows or channels are most at risk?

Our hypothesis is that it's the lower tier of bread-and-butter programming. In other words, it's not top-tier fare. Certainly not *American Idol*, etc. because these shows exist in a rarefied environment of top-tier marketing, and a virtuous cycle of digital engagement (via web, texting, Twitter, etc.) that reinforces the brand and helps retain audiences. The brands of those shows are powerful enough and well-heeled enough that they can and do pursue a multiplatform agenda that hundreds of others shows and channels cannot afford.

Our two illustrative ratings tables ("Illustrative Sweeps Week Ratings (P2+)" and "Illustrative Daytime Cable Ratings (P2+)") demonstrate that rich-poor gap rather dramatically, and show that bread-and-butter channels and shows are likely to be within the economic envelope of the hypothetical digital scenario we just walked through, and with roughly comparable economic implications.

Illustrative Sweeps Week Ratings (P2+)

Show	Network	Rating
American Idol (Tues.)	Fox	31.2
American Idol (Wed.)	Fox	28.9
House	Fox	26.0
Grey's Anatomy	ABC	25.8
CSI	CBS	22.7

Exhibit II-12: Illustrative Sweeps Week Ratings

Illustrative Daytime Cable Ratings (P2+)

Network	Weekday Rating
Lifetime	0.67
History	0.66
FoodTV	0.61
Discovery	0.61
FX	0.59
TVLand	0.54

Exhibit II-13: Illustrative Daytime Cable Ratings

And commercial TV's internet ads sell at very respectable unit prices with every prospect of significant price premiums for superior demographics, sharper targeting, and greater measurability, as the digital audience gradually grows and programmers get a better handle on what to do.

So, in television today any gap between analog and digital is one of dollars to, in a worst-case scenario, somewhat fewer dollars. Not pennies. This (smaller) gap's existence is due not to some inherent "Law of Digital Economics" but to a few prevailing, practical factors and conditions in today's television business as we outlined above.

We've taken a quantitative look at the long-term effects of audience fragmentation that have accumulated over more than twenty years of cable channel proliferation. What we've shown is that, well before the internet came along, cable channels proliferated and audiences in turn fragmented as the heyday of broadcast network television began to wane.

The good news, as we'll explore in Chapters IV and V, is that these very same "have not" channels are also more likely to benefit from well-designed, affordable internet presence which helps stabilize and improve the reach of the linear product. In other words, the internet can be used to drive people back to watching regular TV, not just for siphoning off viewers from the living room to the laptop.

That's enough numbers for now about where we are. Let's turn next to the qualitative effect that television's evolution is having on viewer behavior and begin outlining some of they key problems with today's "user experience," to steal a term from the software industry. That will wrap up our overall assessment of the current situation, and then lead us to discuss what viewers want in the next chapter, followed in turn by how to economically deliver it to them.

Fragmentation: From Channels to Programs

A television channel was once simply a slice of government-licensed electromagnetic spectrum via which programmers broadcast, free-to-air, whatever it is they had on offer. Over time, channels and day parts became the main way viewers understood and connected with how television programs competed for their attention.

Channels themselves developed brand identities, however transitory or short-lived: Eons ago CBS was "the Tiffany network", or Fred Silverman's ABC of the '70s was about fun but trashy and escapist "jiggle TV", or Brandon Tartikoff's revitalized NBC was the "edgy" FX of its day (*Hill Street Blues, Miami Vice*), or the early MTV really was "music television."

Channels and their daypart and seasonal schedules have functioned much the way newspapers have as the dominant structure and medium for organizing, reporting and presenting news, or as department stores once did as the preeminent way of organizing, presenting and selling a broad range of goods at large scale. A prominently branded store like Bloomingdale's or Marshall Fields could be counted on to merchandise with a certain style, point of view, price range, etc., and customers shopped there with that in mind. While the merchandising analogy is crude, a channel was once a brand too in the same general sense.

Today, the value of channels has largely eroded, not only because there are so many of them, but also because channels seems to be overhauling their identity and focus more and more often, even as program schedules become more unpredictable. So whatever brand associations might exist are often too weak to help viewers with program discovery and selection, and are therefore much less useful to advertisers as an access point to predictable audience sizes and demographics.

Even narrowly-focused niche or "enthusiast" channels struggle with the challenge of brand identity and content discovery. Who really remembers if that upcoming program they heard about on secret tunnels under Old Jerusalem was going to air on PBS, Discovery, the History Channel, History International, the Travel Channel, Hallmark, Ovation, or NatGeo? Which channel is *Ice Road Truckers* on anyway, and is it the same one as *Deadliest Catch*? (Answers: they may both take place in Alaska, but the first is on the History Channel, and no, the second one is on Discovery).

In our view, comparatively few channels have an understandable, memorable brand that's going to be useful to a viewer thinking about what he or she is in the mood to watch. So increasingly, viewers have little to guide them besides already-established loyalty to particular shows or a blizzard of on-screen electronic program guide technology that comparatively few viewers can adequately use, never mind master. And despite the torrent of promos, interstitials, pop-up crawls and all manner of clutter, viewing behavior has become so sporadic that much of that desperate, brute force marketing effort is wasted and forgotten, if not overtly filtered out.

As is probably already apparent, we don't believe existing technology-based solutions purporting to solve the problem of discovering, and then actually finding or locating, programs of interest have proven to be much of a solution at all. Former FCC Chairman Michael Powell famously referred to TiVo (and by implication digital video recorders or DVRs generally) as "God's machine." And there's no question that, if you work these machines hard, you can use them to significantly shift television viewing from a passive, "whatever I randomly come across" channel-surfing experience to one in which the viewer actively becomes his or her own programmer.

In reality, DVR-like functionality, including cable video-on-demand, has fallen well short of the mark in allowing the average viewer to (a) know, and (b) impose his or her interests and will on the stream of programming that emanates from the television set. This is for three reasons.

First, and despite a widespread push by both cable but especially satellite services, DVRs aren't all that widespread. Almost 70% of US television households don't yet have a DVR.

Secondly, of the 30% or so that do, our complete swag of an estimate is that easily half of those have no idea how to use the advanced features to find and schedule their viewing in a consistent, meaningful way - i.e. for half of DVR users, it comes close to having an old VCR sitting under the TV, blinking "12:00." So now we're down to around 15% of television households in control of their viewing.

Third, the DVR-like functionality of video-on-demand has failed to take the market by storm. Let's be generous and say about half of US television households have digital cable (the current technical prerequisite for VoD – the satellite guys, including BSkyB in the UK, are still trying to figure this one out). Therefore, only half the TV households potentially have the convenience of watching what they want, when they want, at least for whatever's in the VoD library. But most of them don't - according to Leichtman less than two-thirds of those self-report being regular VoD users.

Cable companies have become cagier (could there be a problem?)

about releasing VoD buy rate information other than of the "billions viewed" sort of generalities. But we already know that buy rates decline rapidly after initial experimentation. And if viewers were going wild with the convenience of VoD, you can be sure we'd be hearing about it. As with the DVR, slogging through the set top interfaces to find, select, and view what they want, isn't for most viewers.

So netting it out, less than half today's television households are capable of using the inadequate "advanced" multichannel TV viewing tools they've been given. We're not only a ways off from Television Everywhere, we're not even coping with the television industry's pre-internet reality of complexity and missed opportunities.

US "advanced" TV HH

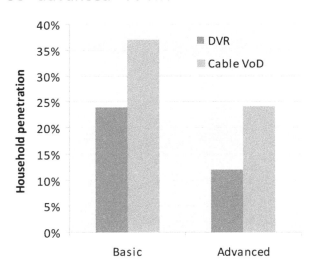

Exhibit II-14 US "Advanced" TV HH

Television's Future

Television as we know it is under threat. The internet is going to change television. It's just not doing much of it yet, or nearly as quickly as "experts" claim. In the long run, television and the internet will combine to form a different medium. In the meantime, however, the relative vibrancy of the television industry and the arrival of internet-delivered video are creating an opportunity. At minimum, to slow the potential erosion of a huge and healthy industry, and at best to expand the business with economics very similar to today's.

In the following chapter, we're going to go back to basics and first principles. We'll examine what it is that needs to be done to systematically improve today's viewing experience, given the complexity, fragmentation, and constantly-changing nature of programming supply, and discuss the (largely positive, in our view) implications for suppliers of television programming.

III. What Viewers Want

How Did Watching TV Become This Hard?

P EOPLE LIKE WATCHING TV. A good deal of what they like are the comforting behaviors and circumstances that go with it – the couch, the drink, the escapism, the passive relaxation or the socializing – that are only indirectly associated with what's actually on the screen.

Most people watch Top 10 fare, live events, have another favorite show or two and, outside of that, often aren't that choosy or particular. Back when there were three networks, and in larger markets a few UHF stations, that arrangement suited viewers and programmers just fine. But now, available commercial video content has mushroomed by two orders of magnitude, and viewers are bombarded by vast amounts of mind-numbing marketing that tries to rise above the din, while actually just making it louder.

Viewing behavior is stuck somewhere between the Three Network era and what's technically possible today. It's not that viewers don't want to watch something "better", i.e. more directly related to their personal interests and tastes. Many viewers know (i.e. have some low-level ambient awareness) that there's very likely more interesting stuff on sometime, somewhere. But they have neither the time nor inclination to try to find it, or don't know how to go about it, or forgot the name of something they heard about at the office, or all of the above.

Part of the rationale is "if it's a show I'll like, it'll come to my attention soon enough somehow." Or not. This is what perpetuates huge and hugely inefficient promotional spending, while dooming much of the programming on mid- to lower-tier channels to a Catch-22 of near invisibility, and borderline profitability. It's a sprawling and massively expensive Off Off Broadway ghetto of shows hoping to carve out an audience niche while dreaming the showbiz dream of becoming the unexpected hit. It's one thing for finding an audience to be a Darwinian process, another for it to be just massively wasteful.

That's the "macro" side of how watching television has become work. Viewers want more or better but aren't finding it. Suppliers languish in the sea of four hundred channels, hoping their shows might be noticed the next time a viewer flips through People magazine or pays attention to an onscreen pop-up promotion.

The "micro" side is the truly awful user experience of getting the program you want actually on to your television screen. And, in circular fashion, micro helps perpetuate the macro problem of poor program discovery. Even if you're motivated to broaden your viewing experience, who wants to learn and fight all kinds of contraptions in order to (maybe) do that?

Many of us know the scene: three or four incompatible remote controls sit on a coffee table, each competing to have the largest array of mispositioned, variously-colored and shaped buttons. One of the buttons on one the remotes turns on the TV.

Exhibit III-1 60 Buttons and Who Knows What's On?

On screen there is a series and hierarchy of menus, spanning what's on now, what's on in the next couple of hours, what you might have recorded in the past, what's available "on demand", what you might like to do to change the functions of the menus themselves, and so forth. Press the wrong button ("Guide"? "Program"? "Menu"? "Info"?) and you're catapulted into screens where you're suddenly groping for the "Exit" button. If you pressed the wrong button too many times in haste or frustration, sit back while the flashing subsides, and start over.

If you want to resort to brute force channel surfing, you'll probably have to forget that too. There are several hundred channels and many of today's "advanced", software-heavy set-top boxes have so much latency (i.e. the delay between pushing a button to do something, and having it happen on the screen) that you'll either never get to, or go way past, your channel destination.

So at best, today's electronic program guides (EPGs), put a complex interface in front of a fire hose of information against which it is very difficult for viewers to overlay their interests and preferences and so, most often, they give up or vastly underutilize the available features due to their complexity

Filtering the firehose of channels...

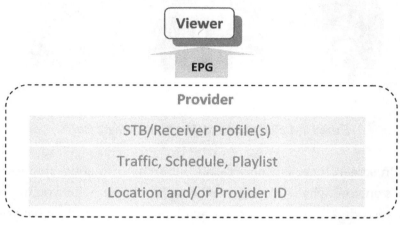

Exhibit III-2 Filtering the Fire Hose

Marketplace and User Experience

The macro, or *marketplace* problem (huge disconnects in connecting viewers with programs) and micro, or *user experience* problem (delivery and user technology which only adds to TV's sprawling complexity) converge in the majority of American living rooms every day. If you're a viewer, it's too hard to discover, locate and organize what you like to watch. If you're a supplier, it's too hard, too hit-or-miss, and too expensive to find, attract and retain audiences, and the window in which to do so continues to shrink. Programs disappear unknown, unsampled, unwatched, into a zombie world of brand and channel clutter, schedule confusion, and unreached audiences, just like the advertising that pays for them.

With channels no longer able to adequately provide the branding and merchandising mileposts that viewers once relied upon, the TV viewing experience has turned into the living-room equivalent of a trip to the Marrakech Souk in Morocco, but without a guide.

Intriguing, endless, colorful, sometimes frightening labyrinths of stalls and shops, their merchants all clamoring for your attention and making loud, incessant, and questionable claims for your business.

In this chapter we'll look inside the marketplace problem and, after first breaking it into pieces, offer some solutions. We'll also discuss the user experience problem, at least in terms of alternative, much better-suited technologies and approaches. These technologies – mixes of which are seen in things like Google Apps or the iPhone App Store – are well adapted to improving the viewer and supplier experiences for each of the components of television viewing we describe below. These technologies, while in no way solutions in and of themselves, have the added benefit of being architecturally simple, bite-sized, inexpensive, and not under the hegemonic control of today's major television distributors (e.g. cable and satellite companies) or their captive technology suppliers.

The unifying theme underlying our discussion of both challenges – macro/marketplace, and micro/user experience – is the idea that watching television has become an "application" – an involved, multi-step process. The task of watching TV long ago began shifting from turning on the TV, setting the dial to a channel, and flopping down on the couch for the next hour. This evolution, the complexity of channel count and technology layers it has accreted, has been so gradual and so long-standing that few have stopped to do a clean-sheet re-examination of what's going on.

There's no changing the underlying complexity – that's simply a fact of life. But what is possible is for content providers themselves to explicitly recognize the challenges, and help viewers cope with, simplify, and get what they want out of the exploding marketplace of commercial video, no matter what the delivery "platform." And, with the availability of a whole new generation of low-cost technologies, both macro and micro problems can be addressed jointly.

Before we do a deconstruction of TV watching into application-like parts, let's first think about key elements that might be on today's viewer wish list, and get to that by thinking about common situations (or, in software parlance, "use cases") where viewers need help, for example:

- What happened on the last *Gossip Girl* ?

- Missed the last episode of *Mad Men,* it's mid-week and I need to catch up before Sunday.

- Are there any good documentaries on Egyptian mummies?

- I need to build up a library of commercial-free preschool kids shows

- There's some new HBO series starting in the summer – forgot the name, but need a reminder when that happens because usually HBO has stuff I like

- I liked that last *Myth Busters.* Any more shows of that sort I might like?

- Let me click on this Tweet and get to the show, segment, or clip I'm being referred to.

- I think Jack would really like that *Saturday Night Live* sketch – I need to get it to him

- I'm ready to resume watching that home improvement show I started while I was in that taxi stuck in traffic

- Just line up a bunch of cooking and travel shows about Italy for me, especially ones with personalities I like (Anthony Bourdain, Giada DeLaurentiis, Lidia Bastianich, for example)

… and many others are possible, but this list will give us a diverse enough mix of requirements to think about. Let's raise the bar a bit further by specifying some of the technical characteristics our hypothetical viewer brings as well:

- Has digital cable in three rooms, one cable box is also a DVR, another is not, and the third has no set top (i.e. cable is a direct input to the television, so premium channels requiring conditional access technology are not visible)

- Broadband at home, mainly WiFi

- Has an iPhone or Android phone

- Carries a laptop from time to time

- Is a registered user on Hulu and YouTube

- Has a Roku/Netflix box attached to the living room television set for streaming some Amazon and Netflix programming, but is also a "regular" (ie. DVD rental) Netflix subscriber

Television As "Application"

We've set the scene, now let's define the six-part framework for television viewing while keeping our representative viewer situations and home technologies in mind.

Starting at the beginning, watching (especially linear) commercial video content has a number of steps, from figuring out and remembering what's out there, to being rewarded for loyalty to a show, with a number of steps in between. Viewers go through this cycle repeatedly, which is shown in the "Television as Application" diagram:

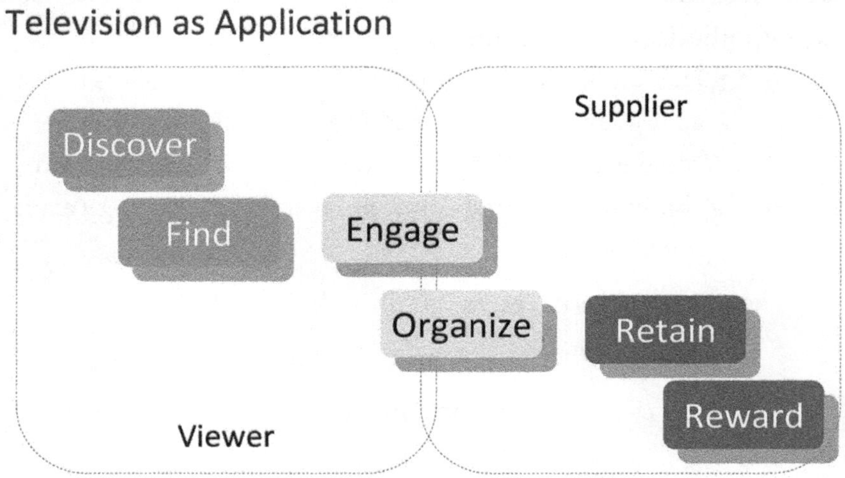

Television as Application

Exhibit III-3: Television as Application

- *Discover:* becoming aware of a program or series. This is done via anything from on-air promos and interstitials to ads on the side of a bus.

- *Find:* Actually locating an "airing" of a program across whatever delivery format the viewer would like or has access to (linear, VoD, DVR recording, internet stream, etc.). "Finding" means turning a general, often vague awareness of a program into the actual intent and ability to watch (what time, what channel, what website, etc., etc.)

- *Engage:* at minimum, actually watching. At maximum, the sky's the limit: sharing with friends via Facebook, buying related merchandise, texting votes about contestants, you name it.

- *Organize:* making it possible for viewers to organize, schedule, manage, prioritize, and otherwise control their viewing – and this is key – *regardless of medium or platform*, i.e. whether on Hulu, YouTube, cable, over-the-air, on the "phone". Preferably this is an active capability - it schedules it for you, reminds, you, saves it for you, whatever.

- *Retain:* at the end of the day, if a viewer doesn't like a show, he or she won't keep watching it. Or, if the show's a *Mad Men*-level cultural phenomenon, viewers will find a way to keep watching without much prompting. But the vast majority of TV falls into the grey middle between love it or hate it, with a likelihood of missed episodes and generally drifting away. The better suppliers do at Engage, Find, and Organize the better they will do at viewer retention. But it also involves occasional and creative communication to retain interest. And motivation ("Reward", below)

- *Reward:* When it comes to rewards, TV has two things going for it. People appreciate rewards in the form of more TV and less commercials ("watch tonight's *Anthony Bourdain's No Reservations* and get a one-day unlimited pass at Hulu Premium Edition"), and those rewards cost very little (vs., say, inserting a breakfast cereal sample into a Sunday paper delivery).

As we show in our "Television as Application" diagram, the first steps (Discover, Engage) are mainly viewer-driven activities, the last (Retain, Reward) are mainly supplier-driven (e.g. channel, show) activities, and the middle (Engage, Organize) is where the rubber meets the road and viewer and supplier get actively connected. Another way of thinking of this framework is as a sieve or filter which can catch and stop potential audience "leakage" at each step.

Instead of viewing the internet as a threat, *each* of these steps can be helped along by tools using today's technologies and approaches to applications to transcend and radically simplify the world of 60-buton remotes and multi-layer menus. There will be "an app for that."

As we'll also see, there's (a) an opportunity to support each of these steps as part of a single "application", not as one-off tools, and (b) the possibility to integrate, over time, access to and control over multiple platforms, not just linear TV itself. In other words (again, over time) this framework can be used to think about marketing, viewing, and retention activity no matter what the "touchpoint" (e.g. device, type of screen), or delivery method (Hulu, Netflix, YouTube premium, broadcaster website, cable, satellite, etc.)

At the center of the TV-as-application notion is rebalancing the viewer/supplier relationship. Today, programmers direct a one-way fire hose of options towards the viewer, and offer complex, largely incomprehensible tools with which to filter and impose priorities and order.

Our view is that it should be a two-way balance in which (a) viewer interests, history, and diverse program sources are an integral part of the discovery process and viewing prioritization, and (b) the technical implementations are less complex and provider-centric (e.g. the "big bang" vertical network implementations from cable, etc.)

Watching what you want...

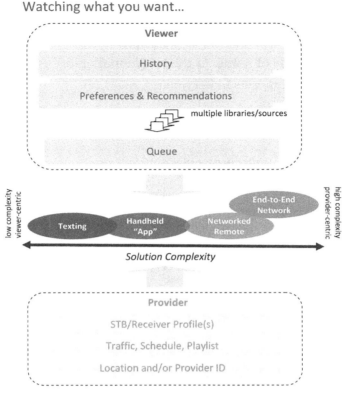

Exhibit III-4 Watching what you want – balanced view

Next, we're going to get more specific about how to do some of this, so we'll transition from talking about an application as a metaphor for the process and general complexity of watching TV, and shift to talking about high-level requirements for simple, but actual software. So we'll refer to the hypothetical software application as "HelpView" to differentiate if from the broader application metaphor.

HelpView: There's an App for That

By far the hardest problem to solve in the six-part application framework is seizing the fleeting, but very valuable moment when a viewer becomes aware of something that might be of potential interest later on. As we noted in our brief description above of 'Discovery', that interest might be piqued from anything from a poster on the side of a bus, to the traditional on-air promo, with a wide range of situations in between.

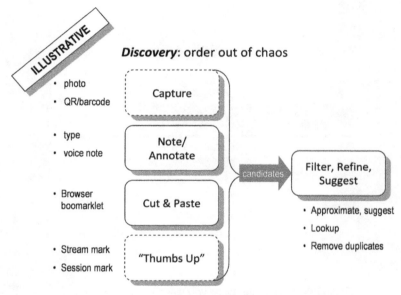

Exhibit III-5 Discovery: Order out of chaos

In the diagram 'Discovery: order out of chaos' we propose four kinds of discovery situations that HelpView can support:

- *Capture*: Real-world, "augmented reality" situations like the poster on the side of a bus, a QR or barcode on a piece of promotional collateral, magazine ad, or even on-screen display. HelpView should enable capturing an image (imagine a smartphone camera) and then sending it off to be decoded and digested to the extent possible.

- *Note/annotate*: allow for the viewer to type or make a voice note, say, "show about garbage" (*Garbage*

Moguls, perhaps?) and pass the note forward to be made sense of by HelpView's discovery "engine"

- *Cut & paste:* select text from another source (browser, email, tweet, or a text message) and pass it downstream

- *"Thumbs Up":* a TiVo-like ranking function to mark something being mentioned in a viewing stream or a linear TV viewing session, and passing it on for later review

The first, "upstream" case (Capture) and the last, "downstream" case (Thumbs Up) are together by far the most complicated and would need careful experimentation to make sure complexity doesn't overwhelm utility, nor swamp the simpler aspects of the discovery-helping functions.

In all cases, the candidate snippet of discovered programming interest is captured and passed forward to a discovery engine which tries to sort out and make sense of what is being provided, using localized traffic systems, IMDB-like databases, collaborative filtering across other application users, and so forth. So a note simply saying "show about garbage" results in a bunch of refinements and database lookups that suggest NatGeo's *Garbage Moguls* as a likely possibility.

The overriding idea is to be able to deal with almost any impulsive, fleeting discovery opportunity. HelpView would enable the viewer to capture them easily no matter what the medium or situation, and store them so that the application can interpret what they mean and suggest specific programs. Having created, over time, a list of interests and candidate programs, the viewer can then later refine and organize his/her viewing preferences. We make a distinction between discovering and finding, because even if, say, the viewer identifies *Garbage Moguls* as the target program of interest, that still-general definition must be translated into a specific episode, channel number or web episode/clip before actual viewing action can be taken.

There are two follow-on, on-going benefits to the HelpView-enabled discover/find process. In addition to translating a weakly-formed or weakly-expressed interest into a specific viewing opportunity, HelpView becomes a habitually-used tool the viewer is routinely engaged with (i.e. the very reliance on the application becomes part of the 'Retain' step in our framework). HelpView becomes one of the primary points of contact whereby

- the viewer gets progressively more connected, and directly so, with programming providers

- even if many of the discovered programs turn out to be later rejected or ignored by the viewer, those selections shape an important profile of what's on the viewer's mind and where his/her interests lie in a broader sense (genre, theme, etc.). It would function in much the same way as Netflix's record of subscriber selections, combined with occasional ratings, to hone the sense of what the viewer wants.

Which leads us to a second, simpler model of discovery and one which could either complement what we described above, or substitute for it.

Pandora TV

Earlier we mentioned "collaborative filtering" (or CF). Broadly speaking, CF is an approach to rummaging through a wide array of diverse data sources from multiple different points of view to isolate useful patterns. The computer science technologies to do so have evolved from large-scale analyses of everything from seismic exploration data to consumer financial records.

Most of us experience CF via things like Amazon or Netflix

recommendations, where our purchases and preferences are analyzed with regard to "like" sorts of customers, enabling educated guesses as to what we might like to buy next.

While there are early-stage companies (TV Genius, for example) seeking to apply CF as part of a smart recommendation system for watching television, most of what we've seen or heard about so far seeks to either:

- embed the discovery capability in a complex array of extant electronic program guide (EPG) and set top systems, or

- force the viewer to interact with a recreated version of a localized online TV guide (think, again, 60-button remote) to input and capture preferences in ways we've never managed to fathom.

Finally, there were early efforts, such as TiVo's recommendation feature that produced vast and random-seeming lists of shows to the point of prompting a rash of satirical articles of the sort "Does TiVo Think I'm Gay?" because so much off-target stuff (apparently centered on the Bravo channel?) was put on the recommended list.

As we noted earlier in the chapter, the long-standing concept of a linear television channel barely works any more as a mechanism for effective program discovery. Starting with the viewer in mind, CF technology could allow users to recreate the channel concept by, in effect, programming their own much more easily and effectively than any of the popular technologies (notably including the DVR) permit today.

An analogy for this internet-era recasting of custom television channels would be to adapt the concepts behind the popular Pandora internet music streaming service to a kind of "Pandora TV." Pandora employs a combination of human categorization of music, with progressive refinement and narrowing of program choices (thumbs up, thumbs down) as the listener grows accustomed to what a given "channel" offers. Channels can be created from scratch with a few "seed" examples (in Pandora's case songs or artists), or can be selected from existing, public channels shared by other subscribers and then customized by others.

So HelpView might balance a mix of three approaches to program discovery:

- detailed, granular selection of programs (as in the 'Discovery: order out of chaos' exhibit and descriptions above)

- intelligent recommendations based on historical viewing behavior and interests supplemented by collaborative filtering of viewing interests by a growing base of similar subscribers

- pre-fabricated starter channels subject to refinement and filtering by the viewer (i.e. a la Pandora) and possibly by the two mechanisms immediately above

The Decisive Moment

If viewers can't connect their interests with what's actually out there, an enormous amount of programming and advertising goes to waste. Therefore, simplifying and managing the program discovery and finding process is, we believe, the most valuable (and most difficult) part of fixing the viewing experience. Doing so begins the process of modernizing television viewing, helping viewers cope with the fragmented 400-channel universe. For suppliers, fixing discovery is a foundational step on an evolutionary trajectory towards the platform-agnostic (linear, web, mobile) distribution of commercial video which is television's long-term future.

There's one small problem, however. Someone has to push the button. All the promoting, marketing, discovering, and finding comes down to a single event – the actual moment of consumption. As wonderful as it would be to have a managed queue of things to watch, reflecting personal preferences and interests and all manner of custom goodness, how does the stuff actually get watched? There are only two possibilities: the viewer pushes the button to tune it in, or some (software) agent makes it happen on the viewers behalf. HelpView needs to enable both.

There are three ways to transition from Discover/Find to Engage (i.e., at minimum, watch the show) where linear television is involved:

- *Alert*: Let the viewer know when and where to watch – "*Garbage Moguls* starting on Channel 65 (NatGeo) in 10 minutes", alerting on whatever mobile device he/she preselected. A slightly fancier version might be "location-aware" and let you know if, say, you're out of town on business what channel to watch at your hotel, if it's available. The alert could be acknowledged (I'm going to watch), waved off (can't watch, log to queue in case there's a rerun, web episode), or flagged for later (interrupted, note where I left off in case we can do something about seeing what I missed later – clips, highlights, etc.)

- *"Universal remote"*: Change the channel automatically by either having the viewer point the (infrared-equipped) mobile device at whatever set top/TV is the default, or send a signal to a WiFi/Bluetooth-enabled infrared beacon the user has installed near the set top/TV. With some collaboration from satellite and cable providers, scheduling DVR recordings could also be an included function, though it would likely be midway between the sort of remote control behavior we describe above, and open access to an application program interface as we describe immediately below.

- *Middleware + API* (or Application Program Interface): This is the scary case. The first case (alert) involves no extra technology beyond the application itself, and its up to the viewer to grab the remote and do what the alert says. The second case ("universal remote") involves ten dollars of extra technology to relay a command which simulates the remote control.

This third, or "API" case, while technically possible, involves enormous architectural complexity and adaptation to legacy networks and infrastructure so varied and constantly changing, that such a solution is almost guaranteed to fail. The aim of this approach is to sprinkle software ("middleware") throughout the network and devices (set tops, IP-enabled TVs, browsers, handheld operating systems, video servers) in order to bring Television Everywhere to life. And this is the sort of approach to which cable companies, satellite companies, phone companies, and their technology suppliers are instinctively drawn, usually miles away from any sense of or focus on what viewers actually want.

There's a bunch of stuff going on – OCAP, or OpenCable Application Platform, or its "consumer-facing" (?) name tru2way, is a key example – that aspires to integrate and otherwise enable a uniform technical nirvana a la Full Service Network of the early '90s. And perhaps it will someday. In the meantime our view remains: good luck, and let's steer clear of these efforts for now while coming up with simpler, cheaper solutions we can put in viewers' hands today.

Bringing it Together

"Organize" is the part of the application framework where, outside of suggesting a few basic principles, we have the least to say. Much of what HelpView might concretely provide to organize all the viewing choices will depend on how it has been designed to support the preceding steps – i.e. what and how much does it do for predecessor parts of the framework – as well as which "type" of viewer it's aimed at (we'll talk about a simple market segmentation in the next chapter).

We tend to believe a one-size fits all approach (vs. multiple application flavors) probably won't be the right way to go. And, other than to clarify the intent of organizing, using facile metaphors like "dashboard" or "control panel", etc., doesn't actually get us anywhere concrete.

So let's just note three key things HelpView's organizing functions should try to address:

- *Queuing and prioritizing what there is to watch.* There's a wide range of possible lists that need to be managed, from on-going shows a viewer likes, to newly discovered material that is possibly a candidate for viewing, to suggestions from others, linear vs. DVR-stored, vs. web-based content, shows the viewer started watching but interrupted, etc. Somehow the organizing function needs to simplify and sort out the viewers choices in this mix.

- *Keeping track of what has and hasn't been watched:* Viewing history is part of what drives future recommendations and choices. The accumulated record could become a virtual "library" and reference point for sharing content with others, or deciding which promotional or other consideration to offer to the viewer (see below).

- *Incentives and Rewards:* We envision HelpView-style applications as the active bridge between program supplier and viewer. They enable programmers to (re)build direct relationships with viewers which overcome the fragmentation of the content marketplace and the erosion of channel brand power. HelpView's organizing function is where the viewer would shape and modify an existing base of choices and would be a logical place to incorporate presentation of promotions and rewards ("The episode of *MythBusters* in your HelpView viewing queue will be the fifth one you've watched, so we're pleased to offer you...")

Building a Virtuous Cycle

The final two steps in the application framework (Retain, Reward) are about maintaining and strengthening the on-going relationship between the program supplier and viewers that has been built over time, likely through continuous use of HelpView-like applications.

We contend that retention (ensuring the viewer keeps watching a given program, or even linear TV in general) is driven by three things, the last two of which can be influenced by our hypothetical application:

- whether the viewer actually likes the show – not much we can do to influence that beyond maximizing the exposure a potentially interesting show gets from candidate viewers

- avoiding "out of sight, out of mind" – reminders, displaying a 'myTV' queue, etc. can combat forgetfulness, gradual drifting away, and viewer disengagement

- provide higher quality, more continuous engagement – offering clips, highlights, outtakes, talent-authored blogs, to keep the viewer involved and entertained outside of and in between program episodes themselves.

The latter (quality of engagement) is something show-specific web sites or Hulu are particularly good at. But without HelpView-style active intervention, there's little to drive viewer traffic to them other than goodwill, the viewer's own memory, or a hodge-podge of disconnected emails, text messages, etc.

Hypothetical Score Card

Let's wrap up by going back to the specifics of what motivated this discussion in the first place – specific viewer needs and circumstances that our hypothetical HelpView-style application(s) would support.

Viewer Problem	Example HelpView Solution(s)
What happened on the last *Gossip Girl* ?	(if a regularly viewed series) Check the 'myTV' queue for shows in the past – click the episode to be directed to highlight or synopsis clips on Hulu or cw.com Search by show name, highlight *Gossip Girl*, add to "Friend/ Follow" queue, then see above

Missed the last episode of *Mad Men*, it's mid-week and I need to catch up before Sunday	Search/queue highlights as above, or Re-queue for DVR if being rerun during the week, or cable 'Start Over' queue or Add to Hulu, amc.com queue if available for streaming replay
Are there any good documentaries on Egyptian mummies?	Genre search/browse Add to 'myTV' library for
I need to build up a library of commercial-free preschool kids shows	Genre search/browse, filter by channel/network (e.g. PBS group) Add to 'myTV' library (for DVR queue, online, etc.)
There's some new HBO series starting in the summer – forgot the name, but need a reminder when that happens because usually HBO has stuff I like	Check 'myTV' queue, filtered by HBO for promotional announcements Search/browse "coming soon"
I liked that last *Myth Busters*. Any more shows of that sort I might like?	Check 'myTV' queue for watched episode – click/search for "related/recommended"
Let me click on this Tweet and get to the show, segment, or clip I'm being referred to	Cut and paste tweet or bit.ly URL, add to 'myTV' queue Use browser plug-in, click "send to 'myTV'
I think Jack would really like that *Saturday Night Live* sketch – I need to get it to him	Check the 'myTV' queue for previous SNL episode – select from "scenes" then "forward" (sends URL + description + min:secs displacement)
I'm ready to resume watching that home improvement show I started while I was in that taxi stuck in traffic	Select from 'myTV' queue and then "resume on <device>", where available devices are custom selected based on prior profile and program availability

In hindsight, we can now see that most of the situations were of the 'Discover' and 'Find' sort, or at least started at that end of the application sequence. A HelpView-style application would:

- identify the program(s) the viewer is looking for and put them in the custody of a managed, prioritizable queue

- give precedence to linear TV viewing options (including DVR) when possible

- re-engage the viewer with "missed" content by directing them toward highlight or summary clips online (typically Hulu or channel/show-specific websites)

- keep adding to the viewers library or list of defined interests in order to refine future recommendations

Progression: Time + Place + Medium

Over time, HelpView-style applications would become progressively richer in incorporating three key characteristics as completely as possible:

- *time-shifting:* either helping the DVR-equipped viewer ensure the program is recorded for later use, or looking up alternative air times, VoD options, DVD rental, etc.

- *place-shifting:* when possible, giving the user the option to choose which device and location to view a program (e.g. laptop, mobile device, living room, etc.)

- *medium-independence:* the application for managing the viewing lifecycle would itself become increasingly medium-independent. This would enable the viewer to use a handheld device, a browser plug-in, or a DVR software add-in/widget with largely equivalent functions and user experience to manage their viewing activity no matter what device or location. Within reason, HelpView looks and acts the same, no matter what the access point.

The likely way to start bringing HelpView functionality to viewers is via a handheld application (think iPhone, Android, etc.) which simplifies, controls and manages video consumption on any relevant device. This is because smart, handheld devices are comparatively ubiquitous, and are dominated by a few app-friendly platforms and their application marketplaces. Developing for them is comparatively simple and cheap, and applications can be brought to market quickly, and revised iteratively. In short, an "80/20" solution.

The point about iteration is important – program fragmentation and complexity (what's on where, what the windows are, which channel participates in Hulu to what degree, etc. etc. etc.) are only going to get worse as Hollywood and its distributors continue to experiment with new services and digital policies. Adding to the problem, there's unlikely to be a monolithic "Hollywood position" vis-à-vis windowing, the role of on-demand vs. DVD sell-through, etc., thus further complicating viewers lives in the near- to medium-term at least. So the HelpView-style applications will be instrumental in shielding viewers from the turbulence, or at least helping them navigate through it.

Finally, using handheld functionality and technology as the starting point (which can evolve gradually into a multi-platform tool for Television Everywhere) also brings the significant strategic benefit of bypassing complex "big bang" cable-centric architectures. So it not only avoids a technical black hole, it more directly enables content owners (programs, channels, studios) to have strategic control and sponsorship of the supplier-to-viewer relationship.

Function		Bare Bones	Full Featured
Discover		• Pre-fab starter channels	• All four-modes of capture • Starter channels
Find, Engage		• Program queues • Alerts with localized channel instructions	• Program queues • Universal remote
Organize		• Manage queues and discovery preferences	• Integration with "non-traditional" program distribution (e.g. Netflix, Amazon, etc.)
Capabilities	*Time-shift*	• Schedule alerts	• DVR add-in/widget
	Place-shift	• Linear to web when possible	• Multi-device sessions (pause, resume)
	Medium-independence	• Handheld/mobile-centric function • Queue web viewing (bookmarklet)	• (nearly) the same app for web, hand-held, DVR

Exhibit III-6: Evolution of the TV Viewing Application

IV. Hollywood Everywhere

"It's not really about the movie business,
it's about staying in the picture" – Robert Evans

Television and the Internet

TELEVISION AND THE internet will ultimately fuse into a new medium and new delivery technology whose components are largely foreseeable, but whose mix no one fully understands – yet.

In our view we are far from that point, however, and the transition toward it is likely to be gradual rather than sharp. So right now we believe it's more important to use the internet to help viewers and suppliers cope with the world of 400-channel fragmentation than it is to figure out how to turn internet TV into a viable business (though the two problems are actually quite related). The rationale for this priority is three-fold:

- Fragmentation of audiences and viewer attention is a genuine and immediate problem – improving how viewers, channels, and producers cope with it has real economic value

- Addressing fragmentation through the six-part "television as application" framework paves the way toward time-, place-, and device-neutral video distribution of the future, and can be done in a comparatively low-cost, try-it-fix-it, technology-neutral way. Walk before running.

- Hollywood needs to get out front of and away from another round of misplaced cable industry and phone company initiatives ("Television Everywhere"), possibly intercepting or co-opting them later down the road. The television industry also would do well to strengthen itself in advance of possible strategic moves from Apple and maybe Google. They can be expected to unhelpfully treat studios as "just a library" – junior partners in the eventual convergence of the internet and television – while attempting to strip the industry of some of the windowing and pricing control it enjoys across multiple distribution channels today.

Thus far we've avoided a Big Ideas treatment of internet TV. It crowds out practical thinking and is a line of thought which can rapidly lead to Alice-in-Wonderland rabbit holes of vague, grandiose ideas, barely actionable for consultants and "digital strategists" let alone for people who do the real work in the television industry.

Big Ideas often lead to their immediate and often dangerous neighbor: Big Moves. And in the prefatory chapters on industry history we covered the sad, multi-decade track record of M&A, god boxes, and massive spending on specialized networks, largely untethered to common sense understandings of what viewers and advertisers need.

Below we lay out a simple framework for the relationship between TV and the internet. We try to avoid the Big Ideas trap while providing a strategic, big(ger) picture basis to think about future alternatives. Combined with practical steps of the sort we previously defined, the framework sheds light on strategic trade-offs for deciding "how digital we want to be" and how quickly. It also lays the groundwork for the next chapter's hypothetical industry scenarios – another way to get our minds around how the TV vs. internet story might be shaped.

Television is healthy, in sharp contrast with, say, the recording industry by the time Apple swept the boards with iTunes as the de facto legal outlet for digital music distribution. Nor is TV like the newspaper or magazine publishing business which is struggling to right itself, helped (or "helped", depending on your point of view) by Google.

Whether for offensive or defensive business strategy, television's internet challenge, then, is timing and balance – the speed at which it offers alternatives to existing TV rather than whether it does so or not in the long run. At bottom the TV vs. internet "problem" is about managing the tension between the economic constraints of a still-growing industry with a viable business model, versus viewer and supplier needs inadequately served by existing business practices.

Two things force trade offs between the comfort and comparative predictability of today's television business and the uncertain upside of consumer-demanded, internet-enabled business models in the future. They are the basic dimensions to examine when choosing the path towards how digital, how fast:

(1) *Rights and pricing policies*: Windowing is a system of revenue management. Content revenues are sequenced across various forms of distribution rights – first-run exhibition, video-on-demand, syndication, DVD sell-through, and so forth – enabling content creators to charge multiple times for the same content while extending its value over the life cycle. This revenue model permits

extremely costly scripted entertainment to be sold at a loss or breakeven for broadcast exhibition, with profits emerging from downstream resale via syndication, DVDs, etc. If you're not in the TV industry, the way this works is elaborated for you in the Appendix (*Hollywood Opts Out of the Google Economy*).

Complementing this distribution model are carriage fees and, more recently, their broadcast equivalent – re-transmission consent – which help finance the distribution of television programming by cable channels and network affiliates. So there are many parties with strong vested interests in continuing the licensing, distribution, and pricing practices as they exist today.

(2) *Usage behavior and video delivery costs*: A growing proportion of viewers will expect more time- and place-shifted access to commercial video content. This expectation is reinforced by Hollywood's own initiatives (e.g. Hulu, channel- or program-specific video web sites). And, with more video-friendly mobile devices (smartphones, netbooks) and video-capable broadband networks (including wireless) consumers will want to supplement, or altogether bypass, legacy video distribution channels with other ways of getting at commercial video entertainment.

Today's multichannel video delivery infrastructure (e.g. cable, telco video) is part general-purpose broadband network, but also contains video-specific network elements.

For a large cable system, video-specific capital expenditures (mainly head end and the subscriber premises equipment) are between 30-40% of total network capex. The more video goes over broadband, the less cable systems need of the "old" (and expensive) video network capacity and the more cost-disadvantaged legacy video networks become. With something called DOCSIS 3.0, cable networks can be rejiggered (largely with just software) to re-allocate capacity from legacy video to broadband (and hence internet TV), but even so the architecture of these legacy networks is still unlikely to enjoy the same price-performance improvements of, say, cloud-based video streaming over the internet.

So a hypothetical new Hollywood-driven "cable bypass" video delivery business model could have major cost advantages for two reasons. One is the comparatively lower costs of delivery over the open internet as discussed above, the other is the likely substantial reduction in middleman distribution costs (e.g. carriage fees, retransmission consent) paid to today's cable and satellite distribution intermediaries as rights and exhibition windows are gradually changed to be more internet-centric.

The technical analysis of infrastructure costs and substitution is well outside the scope of this book, but we note the issue because it has very big long-term strategic implications, creating the conditions to disrupt and restructure today's television distribution businesses.

Television Everywhere: Cable's End Run to the Internet

Within this two-part framework (rights/pricing, usage/cost), today's "legacy" television business is positioned in the lower left-hand quadrant: windowing and pricing determined by the content owner, delivered over bespoke/video-specific networks (e.g. cable), with multiple intermediaries (cable channels, the MSOs themselves, network affiliates).

Television Everywhere: strategic view

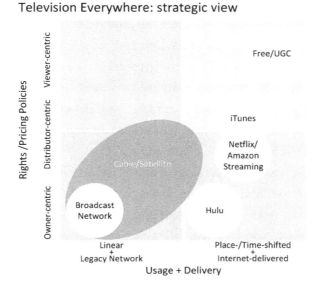

Exhibit IV-1: Television Everywhere – Strategic View

On the other extreme, in the upper right-hand quadrant, is the world of YouTube. Content is largely user-generated (so-called "UGC"), free, and delivered over the open internet.

The center of gravity of today's television business is wholesaling exhibition rights ("owner centric") to channels and/or directly to cable systems, with the distribution chain making money from a combination of advertising and subscription fees. Further up the axis, "viewer-centric" windowing adapts to the convenience needs of small, premium audiences with products such as video-on-demand, or the odd day-and-date releases (which would be comparatively expensive given the potentially significant foregone theater and ad revenue, and the value buyers attach to in-home viewing).

Hulu, a partial compromise between linear television and the world of YouTube, exists in the lower-right hand quadrant. Studios and networks preserve their exhibition rights and control over content, while participating in (and, in some cases, owning a slice of) a consortium which makes selective content accessible via the internet.

Cable, through initiatives under the general rubric of "Television Everywhere" aspires to expand its distribution platform upward and to the right in our matrix, adding progressively more place- and time-shifting ability with internet-delivered content, while attempting to reserve to itself ("distributor-centric" windowing) distribution rights in addition to linear and time-delayed programming (DVR or network DVR features like "Start Over").

There are two barriers to cable's strategic expansion of distribution: extension of exhibition rights to other platforms, and complex legacy network architectures which blend poorly, if at all, with internet-based viewer behavior and program delivery. So cable's strategy for the future relies on three things:

- *Bundling:* by adding on internet access and phone service at a "discount", increasing subscribers' incentives to retain video as the anchor of their relationship with cable systems.

- *Incremental services and access points:* multi-room DVR (record once, watch anywhere in the house), remote DVR scheduling, an assortment of low-cost content giveaways (on-demand exercise videos, whatever) and, recently, complex technical trials of attempts at making "selected" content available on laptops, iPads, etc.

- *Pushing the rights envelope:* almost imperceptibly (video-on-demand) squeezing distribution rights for more "anytime" (if not anywhere) viewing

It's the latter (rights envelope) where Hollywood needs to be at its most vigilant (and automatically will, given the television industry business model). Cable's apparent desire is that, once (or, in our view, a big "if") network technology changes are made, the

TV industry will wake up one day and see that cable commands most of internet TV distribution, both through its end-user access and transport infrastructure, but also with "enhanced" viewing options, for an additional subscription fee, naturally, with a few coins dropped in Hollywood's collection plate.

What the cable industry is banking on is that Hollywood will value comfort with today's distribution arrangements (which do work very well for all parties concerned) over uncomfortable and risky discontinuities and, oh, sure by all means keep playing with that Hulu stuff. In summary, cable would prefer to grudgingly graft on internet distribution while leaving its rich core business largely undisturbed, but at the same time prevent already pesky and disruptive (e.g. Netflix, Amazon, iTunes) clean-sheet distribution models from getting "out of hand", as it were.

Hollywood Everywhere: Digital as We Need to Be

Our view of Hollywood's opportunity is summarized in a parallel chart ("Hollywood Everywhere") in which, within the same framework, we illustrate a television industry "embrace and extend" strategy, levering the exploratory internet presence it began establishing around 2007.

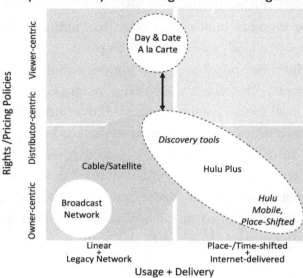

Hollywood Everywhere: migration and endgame

Exhibit IV-2: Hollywood Everywhere

In that view, Hulu (and/or channel- and show-specific web properties like Hulu) expands further to the right to support mobile platforms, and acts as a full-fledged web distributor for more cable channels. HelpView-style application(s) we spoke of earlier are grafted on to the left, enabling viewers to source and manage programs from both linear and internet sources with comparable ease and convenience, but without the false illusion or overblown promises of "seamlessness." This positioning counters and confronts the expansionism of Hollywood's own distributors into internet-based exhibition, while leaving legacy rights intact.

Expanding in these ways – supporting more devices, extending the available library – while keeping most live TV off the internet is a path towards modest subscription revenues for premium features, as well as a systematic defensive play to compete against cable's infiltration of multiplatform TV. Finally, it gives Hollywood the option of an ultra-premium day-and-date release service whose content might be discoverable and managed via the same viewer applications we've discussed for television at large.

How might this play out in the longer run, say in 2020?

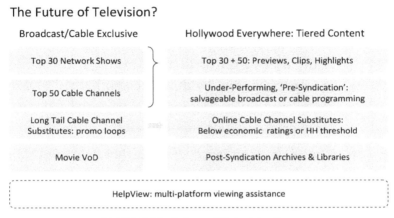

The Future of Television?

Exhibit IV-3: Future of Television?

One possible endgame is that legacy TV and the internet reach a kind of détente or mutual equilibrium in which they co-exist for an extended period. Here's are some illustrative ideas for some of what might happen:

- Cable and broadcast remain the "go to" delivery medium for Top 50 channels and their programs

- Smaller audience channels (i.e. below the hypothetical top 50) move to internet-based distribution…

- … and are replace by a small consolidated set of "now playing" promotional channels that provide previews and highlights that aid discovery of the internet-delivered programming.

- Midseason cancellation of marginal broadcast and cable shows diminishes, and shows are relocated to lower-cost internet-distribution, possibly finding long-term viability if per episode production costs production costs leave reasonable headroom in this alternative distribution model.

- Internet-distribution becomes an integral part of syndication and/or a replacement for DVD sell-through

- Cable infrastructure capacity is reallocated: as many as two-thirds of the linear video channels are removed, bandwidth is reclaimed for 100Mb+ broadband (including internet-delivered video and cable-provided video-on-demand).

- The user experience of "internet-delivered" and legacy network-delivered programming becomes largely identical – with HelpView-style applications, any internet-available program can be "routed" to the living room TV, and so forth.

- Successors of today's cable systems compete with web-based video providers (e.g. Hulu, Netflix) to build ever-larger archival libraries for on-demand viewing.

So we're advocating that Hollywood take strategic control of its internet destiny by focusing on the following agenda:

- *Make order from chaos:* help the viewer sort through the marketplace of commercial video entertainment, no matter what the source. There needs to be a near-Steve Jobsian tyrannical insistence on simplicity and usability ("it just works") vs. the sort of non-starter user experience provided by set top box engineers ("hundreds of features!"). This was discussed at great length in Chapter III.

- *Be in more places:* allow programming to be accessed consistently from multiple devices, but leavened with a dose of common sense – e.g. don't make HD movies available on phones nor create such an expectation for viewers

- *Create derivative content*: Hulu and others already do this to a significant degree – clips and highlights are often valuable entertainment in and of themselves depending on genre (good for, say, SNL sketches, Daily Show rants, or Letterman's Top Ten, not so good for sitcoms or procedurals).

  Derivative short-form content: (a) is a way to get discovered, (b) a money-making (or, more dreadfully, "monetizable") destination in and of itself, (c) a gateway to related long-form content, and (d) keeps the viewer engaged and the brand (show, channel, etc.) going.

- *Make windowing and availability more consistent:* Even on Hulu (especially when including content on other sites linked to from Hulu, e.g. Discovery channels, etc.) the viewer often has little idea as to what he/she can expect to find. Last night's episode? This week's episodes? Earlier this season, but not last season? Stuff from Disney/ABC, but not News Corp./Fox? Hollywood's internet distribution needs to move from ad hoc fragmented experimentation to some form of consistency a user can understand or count on, or the value of a destination site is diminished.

- *One size doesn't fit all:* internet TV usage patterns are still evolving and, it's worth mentioning yet again, still constitute a miniscule fraction of total television viewing time. Within that growing base, however, are very different viewing patterns and needs, as we'll discuss below ('Getting Started')

The NewTV Wish List

One of the things that struck us as we were writing is that a checklist we prepared almost five years ago still holds up reasonably well as a useful reference when contemplating what to do about digital (or as we referred to it then, "broadband") distribution. The general principles above still apply, but it's worth reviewing our 2005 "NewTV Wish List" as a simple tool for assessing where you, the reader, might be and want to go.

NewTV Wish List		Category	Suitability/Example
Incremental revenue	Subscription revenue, advertising, incremental "brand value", etc.	Current season prime time mass audience	Limited; very narrow rights window, value vs. DVR questionable
Contextual sponsorship	New basis for advertising or other contextual sponsorship of content presentation		
Low/no cannibalization	Distinct category of content consumption which does not cannibalize legacy revenues or content rights	Current (1-5 year old) prime time library	Limited; conflicts with syndication and DVD sell-through, BB unable to deliver replacement revenues, value vs. DVR questionable
Optimized viewing	Delivered via quality- and performance-assured network services	Special interest channel	e.g. Hallmark Channel, family; History Channel, hard-to-reach male demos
Content protection	Content rights-holders adequately protected while balancing consumer convenience		
TV endpoint	Can be easily viewed on a television directly connected to the service	BB-friendly premium demographics	e.g. 'The Simpsons' (top 40 share, top 10 CPMs), MTV Overdrive, Comedy Channel broadband sampler
Breakout HH reach	Drives reach to and past the 50M HH level	"We Media"	e.g. Current TV, Link TV; BB-friendly demos, "interactive", mainstream distribution often out of reach
Exclusivity (medium-specific)	Sufficiently exclusive (for the chosen delivery medium) to be valuable and uniquely create traffic?		

Exhibit IV – 4: NewTV Wish List

Let's go down the list:

- *Incremental revenue:* We discussed, at length, in the previous chapter how to look at digital economics. The main truth to focus on here is that it's fairly unlikely that internet-delivery will cannibalize or otherwise be dilutive to most genres of linear programming – yet. So, the answer (to "incremental revenue?") is most likely going to be: "yes, but a small amount for now, and it can be optimized a bit with sensible targeting and discovery" (see 'Getting Started' and 'The Google Economy: Opting Back In', chapter sections below)

- *Contextual sponsorship:* a somewhat regrettable jargony phrase in an attempt to be terse in a chart. But the basic question remains: "can we create additional viewer value we can make money on?" via subscription, higher CPMs due to "engagement" and targeting (see, again, incremental revenue, above). With regard to the CPM question, the honest answer for now must surely be "probably, but we don't know, so we'll try it out." There are massively complex ad research stories out there about "metrics" and various forms of online instrumentation, but if a credible case is being made for today's online audience CPMs, we're unaware of it. Right now, led mainly by Hulu, the market is trying to find its own level as far as commercial load and CPMs are concerned, with Hulu taking the sensible view that the commercial load should be about half of the (often extreme) broadcast model.

- *Low/no cannibalization:* Our thesis here remains: use the internet to drive traffic to linear programming first, and then to internet-delivered programming second, over a much longer term. The answer to the cannibalization danger, however, is surely channel- and/or genre-specific. The folks at Discovery, for example, appear to be on to this, ensuring that next to no full episode content is available online, and that Hulu acts as a simple portal which routes you quickly to Discovery-owned channel and program websites. So they are protecting syndication revenue, trying (within traditional internet marketing means) to use the internet to drum up interest in their TV shows, while making a bit of money off clips and highlights.

- *Optimized viewing:* This might have been a technical issue five years ago, but our view has shifted away from whether it's possible, to selecting from the many possible infrastructure alternatives for how it can be delivered. The advent of cloud infrastructure, whether you use it directly or not, has caused a rapid decline of unit costs for end-to-end internet-based video delivery, as well as a proliferation of technical alternatives and vendors.

- *Content protection:* Five years on, still pretty much a mess, which tends to favor streaming solutions vs. downloads and "owned" digital content. There are quasi-invisible and rather elaborate-sounding industry initiatives on this score (most notably DECE, the "Digital Entertainment Content Ecosystem") but their likelihood of complexity-driven failure remains very high. So the answer here must be based on a combination of "streaming or not" policies, how you feel about iTunes (ahem, Jeff Zucker and NBCU) and Amazon, and windowing policies themselves.

- *TV endpoint:* Watching internet video content on your living room TV is also still pretty much a mess for people of average technical ability and interest, and this slow-changing situation is one of the secondary reasons for our thesis that the internet should drive viewers back to regular old linear TV watching.

Remember that DVRs, despite all the satellite give-aways, etc., are still in barely a third of US TV households, and are way underutilized. The idea of internet-connected TVs rapidly sweeping the country we find far-fetched, and today's consumer electronics fad seems to have switched, at least temporarily, to 3D.

When, however, the percentage of households with internet-connected TVs matches and exceeds the DVR penetration percentage, we'd rapidly concede this is a big deal with big distribution implications. Again, don't hold your breath – it's likely a 2020 thing, not a 2015 thing, in our view.

- *Breakout HH reach:* Here we rather breezily asserted that what we're looking for is the internet-equivalent of the fifty million household rule-of-thumb for reach when, say, new cable channels are looking for carriage. The idea of some minimum economic threshold still feels to us to be conceptually right, but the idea that it is broadly fixed (and so large) is wrong. It's understandable that we'd want to translate internet-based viewing into some TV-like currency that network, channel, and ad executives know and love.

The right answer here seems to be about making rough but credible estimates for "reach enhancement" which includes two elements: (a) reach to non-overlapping (i.e. they don't watch much linear TV) internet audiences based on some segmentation ideas elaborated below; (b) closing the reach vs. the discovery and engagement gap – example: Current TV meets the "50 million" reach threshold but nobody watches it. Why? What can we do to fix it in the context of using the internet to drive both linear *and* internet-based viewing?

- *Exclusivity (medium-specific):* i.e. windowing that dare not speak its name. Common sense tells us that complete distribution parity between live (OTA- or cable-delivered) broadcasts and internet-accessed programming cannot become commonplace without creating total chaos in the existing distribution model. So the trickiest part of the evolution is going to be maintaining (and loosening) windowing rules in which broadcast exhibition has complete precedence. For some mid-tier cable channels, withholding first-run exhibition rights from internet delivery may turn out to be silly and a lost opportunity – the live audiences are already fragmented, why not boost them by whatever means available. But for, say, *American Idol* to be simultaneously live on the internet is nearly inconceivable today – it puts affiliate station agreements, retransmission consent, carriage fees, exclusive ad sponsorship, and all manner of things in economic (and, presumably for now, legal) jeopardy, while also being unnecessary – it's extremely unlikely to create incremental value when the audiences are already so gigantic.

With the checklists above in mind, let's turn next to which audience segments and programming types are the optimal wedge for turning the internet into a complementary delivery channel.

Getting Started

An essential part of determining "how digital we want to be and when" is figuring out for whom.

On the one hand there is the internet's potential advantage as a ubiquitous infrastructure – like over-the-air (OTA) television, nearly everyone could watch, not just those with access to specialized video delivery networks like cable and satellite pay services (although, in the US, pay television households still exceed wireline internet penetration by a tad).

On the other hand, the internet's ubiquity is offset by the fact that making sense of what's available requires smart, application-like, customizable features targeted at the needs of different types of viewers. The internet ocean is simply too big for the average viewer to boil and distill into content of interest, and different viewer types will want to get there in different ways for different reasons.

This means the viewer population needs to be segmented and sequenced in some simple way that reflects their relative interest in digital viewing, starting with their actual behavior. Below is an example of what we mean.

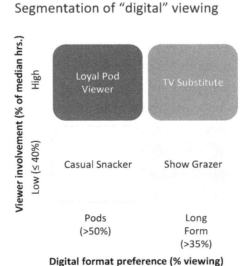

Exhibit IV – 5: Segmentation of Digital Viewing

Our illustrative segmentation divides the internet (i.e. "digital") viewing population in two ways:

- *Degree of "digital" involvement:* what proportion of commercial video viewing is internet-based – we arbitrarily set the "low" threshold at less than or equal to 40%. While making more stuff available on the internet can certainly induce demand, the premise here is that some of the viewer population, for whatever reason (age, demographics, lifestyle, etc.) is more prone or amenable to internet-delivered video consumption.

- *Format preference:* basically, short- versus long-form consumption. The internet has given rise to short-form derivative content (e.g. clips, highlights) as well as, arguably, shortened attention spans (of the form discussed in the well-known Nicholas Carr piece: "Is Google Making Us Stupid?").

Accordingly, we've divided this dimension into "pod"-oriented viewers who consume 50% or more of their total internet video in small bites (say, in segments of 10 minutes or less) versus those for whom longer formats predominate. We stole "pod" from Current TV which appears to have originated the television usage of that that term for their short-form video journalism pieces.

Within these dimensions we named four hypothetical viewer clusters and, elsewhere in a simple quantitative model not in this book, experimented with a range of possible viewing patterns and their potential impact on the shift away from linear TV.

The key takeaway from this simple segmentation is that, say, "Casual Snackers" (viewers who don't use the internet much for video, and when they do prefer short clips) have different needs and viewing propensities (and advertiser value) than, say, the "TV Substitute" segment which is, in essence, populated by hypothetical cable cord cutters who drive almost all of their viewing to the internet. This, by the way, is something which is next to impossible to do at the moment, at least in the US. But in Britain, for example, we may be closer to realizing this possibility.

As we note above, we experimented with a weighted distribution of viewers in this segmentation at several threshold levels to sketch what might happen to linear TV economics as people increasingly drift towards internet viewing.

In other words, we imagined what might happen if TV viewing went from today's 1% "digital" to 15% or even 25%, with a reasonable mix of viewers in each of the four segments. That "weighting" of the segmentation brings with it assumptions about number of video units watched, average commercial load, middle-of-the-road CPMs, and so forth.

It would be tedious to grind through this here, but our bottom line (and, we believe, conservative) finding is that a 15% shift of total household TV viewing to internet-delivered viewing at half the linear commercial load results in high single-digit loss of linear ad revenues.

These are easily replaced or exceeded by a mix of adjustments, including:

- raising the internet commercial load a bit (to, say, 65% of typical primetime broadcast load instead of half)

- more realistic median CPMs which reflect some degree of higher "engagement" and attention for targeted internet-based video viewing

- adding the dreaded but modest subscription fee

Again, keep in mind that a 15% shift is ten to fifteen times higher than current commercial video viewing levels of internet-delivered TV content for the US television audience.

In Chapter II we showed that the basic economic challenge for turning digital "dimes" into dollars was simply scale. For content owners, there is nothing inherently unprofitable about internet distribution. Lower commercial loads are likely to be offset by higher CPMs at comparable scale and significantly lower distribution costs (e.g. eliminated or reduced carriage fees, cost of O&Os etc.).

So we believe that as exhibitors gradually accrete ever larger internet audiences and thus increasingly bypass today's middlemen (e.g. cable, satellite), Hollywood's economics could be as good as ever. But the road to even a 15% audience shift, never mind 50%, is going to be rocky and filled with conflict as it puts stress on altering existing windowing and pricing arrangements with traditional intermediaries.

In the meantime, the US cable industry is already heading towards what it dubs "Television Everywhere" (e.g. some degree of internet-based distribution), and appears to envision an 80%, one-size-fits-all solution for what are hugely different viewer needs. The thinking seems to be: just add computers as another outlet for cable fare. In their rush to force fit today's profitability and business model onto a future one, cable is relegating internet video delivery to the status of yet another feature and incremental charge.

Combine cable's thoughtless view of the user experience with complex new delivery architectures layered on high-cost, legacy video networks. The result, in our view, is the sort of failure that could give Hollywood both the time and strategic upper hand it needs to redefine distribution economics for the future of television.

The Google Economy: Opting Back In

Back in 2005 (see Appendix: *Hollywood Opts Out of the Google Economy*), we discussed Hollywood's reaction to a growing and overblown fear, manufactured by the news media and commentariat, to a "trend" in which Google would parasitically suck the profits out of television just as Google was alleged to be doing to newspapers and magazines (rather than they, through their own inaction, to themselves).

Filed in 2007, Viacom's on-going and recently ripening copyright litigation against Google sped up what would have happened anyway: copyright-protected commercial video content on YouTube was removed. Hollywood successfully enforced its rights over internet-delivered exhibition of its content. Not long afterwards, Hulu emerged.

While it remains a delicate matter, Google is potentially one of Hollywood's best friends.

As we note above in our viewer segmentation, and as studies show, most internet-based commercial video consumption today is for short-form clips. And of course taking all internet-based video into account (mainly the now-cleansed YouTube's "user-generated content"), that is massively the case.

Because clips and highlights are critical to enabling viewer discovery of and engagement with long(er)-form TV content, and because Google is by far the premier destination for all manner of search-driven discovery, there is a natural affinity between Hollywood and Google. Google:

- *can't "steal" content:* Whatever the ultimate outcome of the Viacom litigation (which is focused on backward-looking punitive measures), Hollywood's internet rights remain secure, as discussed in the Appendix.

- *has an insatiable need for more content:* While Google has moved into browsers (Chrome), operating systems (ChromeOS), mobile "platforms" (Android), application environments (Google AppEngine), and applications themselves (Google Apps), the ad-based revenue flywheel centered on "organizing the world's information" remains the core of the business

- *has a big audience:* Google is the only game in town as far as delivering internet-based "audiences" on a scale relevant to the television industry, though maybe Yahoo! and Bing might be roped in as also-rans.

- *has a workable "monetization" model:* They know how to make and share advertising and referral (e.g. click-through) revenues

- *drives traffic to destination sites:* This is inherent in the very nature of what search engines do

- *is already broadening what "search" means:* The search engine is getting better at covering a growing range of semi-structured media (e.g. video, music), and information contexts (e.g. news, blogs, academic research, etc.)

Hollywood can work with Google (or Bing or Yahoo!) to develop a richer discovery engine for TV, sandwiched between HelpView sorts of user experience and applications on top (i.e what the viewer/user interacts with) and Hollywood's own discoverable clip and content library on the bottom.

Easy-to-use discovery and sampling are going to be at the heart of preserving "linear" TV's effectiveness in the face of continued fragmentation and media choice. But they are also at the heart of enabling viewers to transition from linear to internet-based delivery in ways they can understand and control.

With this in mind, in a Google-friendly scenario, video clips and short-form content would continue to have a light commercial load, and content owners and Google would share revenues from both ad views and click-through referrals. Viewer click-throughs from an interesting clip to its originating long-form content would be the flywheel that would gradually scale an internet audience to commercially meaningful size.

One can imagine too, a HelpView style application or set of applications jointly offered by studios and channels through Google's web-based, Android or future ChromeOS application initiatives.

Far from being in competition with Hulu, the content referrals and Google-based apps would be a navigational and discovery complement for studio- or channel-owned video destination sites, and possibly Hulu itself.

This is a rather important point. Discovery and sampling will be important tools with which to build audiences and transition from linear to internet-based delivery. There is too much program diversity, mass market exhortation is simply too expensive, and the very concept of television "channels" has become too ineffective for "brand" based communication alone to improve results.

Or to quote one of our favorite maxims at the rather contrarian Hoffman|Lewis ad agency:

> *"We don't get them to try our product by convincing them to love our brand, we get them to love our brand by convincing them to try our product."*

There is no better medium than the internet itself to enable search, discovery, sampling and, we hope, actual engagement with "the product." Google itself isn't a silver-bullet answer, but it plays such a fundamental role in organizing and enabling access to information it's hard to see why one wouldn't want to try building upon (instead of duplicating) the functions they provide. Despite the dangers, common sense suggests that in the long run its much easier to do this with Google's help than without, and that Google's technical skills (for example, semantic search), not just scale and reach, can bring enormous value.

In our final chapter, 'Scenarios: Television's Future', we'll explore the major dynamics we've laid out thus far – "digital" economics, the tension between rights/pricing and new forms of distribution – by way of a few possible scenarios. We'll take several different views on the nature and rates of industry change and their causes, and look at the possible future of cable.

V. Scenarios: Television's Future

"The future ain't what it used to be" – Yogi Berra

Broadening Our Minds

THE SPIRIT OF this final chapter is to take the ideas and industry forces we've discussed up to this point and have a bit of informative fun by setting them in motion.

Each of the short scenarios are small thought experiments – industry "what ifs." They are not meant to be predictive though surely elements of them will come to pass. They are not mean to be mutually exclusive though some outcomes, by definition, rule out others. They are not meant to be comprehensive – feel free to conjure a few of your own. And while (we think) entertaining, they also have a serious point as a wake up call to what industry changes could be in store.

As a thinking exercise they bring to mind a wonderful scene in the movie *Batman*. The Joker (Jack Nicholson) and his cohorts raid a stuffy museum full of masterpieces. Just as he is about to unleash his thugs', er, disruptive power, a beaming Joker exhorts: "Gentlemen! Let's broaden our minds!" (cue the trademark Nicholson leer).

Live From New York, It's... CBS?!

We hope the folks at CBS will be good sports about this one. We could have picked any US broadcast network for this hypothetical scenario, but chose them for two reasons: (1) CBS's structural separation from Viacom created a comparatively "pure" broadcast play with little in the way of cable properties, and (2) Les Moonves was out there early (2006) and, for a while, often, evangelizing a "cable bypass" future, though it's something he stopped talking about once retransmission consent turned into actual dollars.

Background: sometime around 2012

- Comcast/NBCU merger complete

- CBS drops from the #1 –rated network to #4, its *NCIS*- and *CSI*-driven lead running its natural, cyclical course (think NBC post-*Seinfeld* and *Friends*)

- In 2010, the N.C.A.A. exercised its right to drop out of the final three years of its men's basketball deal with CBS, switching networks

- CBS shed its outdoor advertising division to raise cash

- CBS' extended retransmission agreements with non-Comcast cable operators start to expire and the cable industry begins aggressively conditioning retrans rates on carve-outs for digital (i.e. internet transmission) rights

- Online viewing of commercial programming (i.e. not YouTube cat videos) reaches 5% of HH time spent viewing. This number is quite substantial and bigger than it may seem because we deliberately specified online commercial video content vs., say, today's couple of percentage points or so of *all* online viewing, so as to keep the focus on direct substitution.

Who's Up/Who's Down?

- *UP*: Hulu – 70% of the incremental viewing in the 5% online above is driven by Hulu, not program- or network-specific video sites. Most of it comes from mobile devices – the living room, as yet, remains untouched.

- *UP*: Comcast/NBCU – NBC returns to being the #1-rated network due to, well, we're not that imaginative, but some kind of successful programming, thus giving the newly-combined behemoth extra swagger in assorted negotiations

- *UP*: Apple – launches iTunes in the Cloud, making it easier, cheaper, and more convenient to watch a still-growing library of video fare. Apple squeezes its way into the non-Hulu 30% of the 5% online viewing, joining Amazon and Netflix as a material player in streaming as well as downloaded video.

- *DOWN*: CBS itself – CBS is increasingly in a three-way financial squeeze: less broadcast revenue due to lower ratings; not even incremental digital ad revenue because they are still largely shut out of (or shut themselves out of) Hulu; other revenue-producing assets (e.g. outdoor) already sold off.

The bottom line: CBS undergoes a sharper than usual cyclical downturn – the "normal" downturn as programming leadership inevitably shifts to someone else, but an additional downturn as trends hostile to broadcast begin to take firmer hold: online viewing and additional industry concentration. In the latter case, Comcast takes the natural opportunity to kick a competitor when it's down, and hard.

Actions

- CBS belatedly cuts a deal with Comcast dominated, yet "independent" Hulu. CBS fare appears not on "prime-time" landing pages but in searchable yet non-obvious zones of the website, clearly relegated to second-tier status.

- CBS makes belated bids for a few cable channels it can ill afford in hopes of strengthening both the top line and negotiating leverage for carriage and retransmission deals.

- CBS announces a "transformational" change: selling off (remaining) O&Os; renegotiating affiliate agreements; auctioning off significant spectrum assets under the delayed/revised FCC so-called reclamation program; building a programming war chest through major cost reductions and spectrum asset sales; a shift to "internet-centric" delivery of as much live programming as possible via CBS.com and TV.com with a strong emphasis on mobile viewers.

The bottom line: CBS tries a Hail Mary pass – beginning the move to a "stationless network" and moving to "cable bypass" not in a stealthy and incremental way, but in a sharp discontinuity, while aiming to preserve cable carriage. In many respects it's not so much bypassing cable as it is becoming a cable station over the internet despite being a broadcast network.

Inhibitors/Consequences?

- As always, in our view at least, the key inhibitor of any "internet-centric" shift, transformational or otherwise, is unwinding or clarifying the constraints of existing exhibition, syndication, and carriage rights.

The scenario assumption is that CBS can move much live programming to the internet by fiat. That could be true for some programming, increasing amounts of it in fact, but how much? For example, we know internet rights to extremely lucrative live sports events are being ever more tightly circumscribed by the owning consortia (NBA, MLB, NFL, N.C.A.A., et al), so we can strike them from the list. How much of the prime time slate might be eligible? How many of the horses have already left the barn – i.e. where producers retained these rights for later "syndication" on their own or cutting their own deals directly with cable.

- Even the reduced CBS of this hypothetical scenario would still be a major player in the commercial video landscape, however. Enough to shake it up quite a bit. Among the (sometimes conflicting) consequences of this hypothetical, transformational move might be:

- Rights holders wake up to "internet broadcast" as a real thing and try to systematically (a) carve it out, and (b) figure out what it really means (probably in that order) in regard to existing windowing slots for first-run exhibition, VoD, syndication, etc. We're hardly "in the mix" re how rights conversations go, but we've been surprised in informal and anecdotal discussions with entertainment lawyers, for example, by how little attention is apparently even now being paid to these issues in programming deals.

- Cable lashes out at what it (probably rightly) perceives as an existential threat and doubles down on its (probably by then clearly failing) Television Everywhere initiatives. Predictably, there is much cranking up of legal machinery which makes the brinksmanship of last-minute station blackouts during carriage negotiation seem tame.

- Hulu's tacit "no live programming" boundary breaks down. Either pressured by shareholders, or as a competitive response to CBS, Hulu debuts live or marginally-delayed (hours, not days) "selected" programming, inching ever-closer to full TV distribution.

The bottom line: the scenario offers one vision of a trigger that might have the effect of shocking the industry out of its incremental drift towards the internet by upending a number of the standard "givens." For example: Internet rights as small, ancillary things. Stations (like "channels") as an unquestioned fixture of broadcast television distribution and its economics. The very difference between "broadcast network" and "cable" channels. And so on.

*　　　*　　　*　　　*　　　*

Nielsen Nirvana

Imagine a world in which not only actual viewing behavior, but viewing preferences, interests, and referrals to friends can be tracked, analyzed, and correlated. Imagine regularly-surveyed panels of viewers by whatever income- or geo-demographic segment you would like. Imagine the ability, with the viewers' permission and active cooperation, to do nearly limitless cluster and conjoint analyses blending in-depth lifestyle profiles with TV preferences. And imagine the ability to create segment profiles which integrate viewing behavior across all viewing "touch points": linear TV, pay-per-view, mobile, and internet.

To quote "Bob Ryan", the thinly-veiled Robert Evans character from HBO's *Entourage*, "Is that something you might be interested in?"

We've just described a multi-billion dollar form of secondary value that flows from implementing the six-part Television as Application framework described at length in Chapter III. Like cable and its Television Everywhere, the advertising and consumer measurement industry has its own long and failed history with its own Holy Grail: instrumenting and measuring consumer behavior for targeted advertising and direct marketing.

Like cable and telcos, marketing and advertising's next-generation, technology-saturated solutions have always been just around the corner. Consumer products companies, ad agencies, and marketing consultants, have spent (or charged) billions on brute force "data mining", couponing, instrumentation of devices from super market scanners to set-top boxes, designing the "store of the future", all in a quest to capture what the consumer "really" wants.

This scenario imagines a different path to a modest, but practical form of the same goal, hypothetically using Nielsen as the poster child for a shift in measurement and analysis that enables ground-breaking changes in advertising effectiveness.

Background: sometime around 2012

- This book made the rounds in upper-middle management at a few studios, channels, TV web portals, ad agencies, and "tenpercenteries" and was roundly ignored

- Nielsen is still slogging through the delayed national conversion of diary markets to metered markets and still reorganizing its multiplatform or "advanced digital" audience measurement services

- 'Canoe', the cable industry project for targeted ad inserts and, to some extent, audience measurement, collapses again

- Google's TV ad sales program remains in limbo, becoming little more than an adjunct spot market for remnant inventory – Spot Runner without the content

- The effectiveness of "social media" advertising continues to be debated, with major consumer brands still not allocating much in the way of media spend to Facebook et al. Each year the debate is refreshed by yet another Old Spice-style "breakthrough" campaign proving, once again, that TV advertising is dead, even as it continues to grow.

Who's Up/Who's Down?

- *UP*: Nielsen – despite market unrest and Nielsen's inability to deliver the Holy Grail, they retain their market leadership as, effectively, the only choice for audience measurement

- *DOWN:* cable systems fail to expand localized/ regionalized advertising inventory because new ad network and placement projects continue to fail, even as market complexity increases

- *UP:* broadcast networks and major cable channels (e.g. USA, TNT, etc.) continue to grow ad revenues since no substitute for raw audience scale (see cable point above) has materialized to simplify media buying in a fragmented television market

- *DOWN:* "digital" agencies

- *DOWN:* major consumer packaged goods manufacturers are increasingly frustrated with the ad market; they threaten to band together to "create alternatives", but don't know how

Actions

- An obscure software development team buried somewhere in the Nielsen organization accidentally picked this book out of the garbage near a copier on a floor where they happened to have offices next to a mid-sized cable channel

- A renegade Nielsen team implements a small iPhone app, tied to a modest traffic (i.e. program guide) database along the lines of the HelpView-style applications we profiled in Chapters III and IV.

- The prototype is demonstrated as a "concept front-end" at a Nielsen annual customer conference in front of increasingly restive accounts still waiting for integrated audience measurement and ad effectiveness products.

- Nielsen constructs ten national consumer panels, giving away iPhones preloaded with the app and paid subscriptions to Hulu and Netflix' broadband service. The panel members are vetted by phone interview and use a private website to provide additional income demographic and other lifestyle information

- Nielsen builds and analyzes one year of HelpView-driven consumer/viewer data and sells multi-million dollar service subscriptions to the top 5 US consumer packaged goods companies and their ad agencies

- Etc., etc. (okay, we've had our fun)

The bottom line: the scenario is about secondary, but still large, value. Nielsen doesn't particularly care if viewers get to see the shows they "really" want, or whether smaller channels with fragmented audiences can more effectively reshape their relationship with viewers. But Nielsen (or an insurgent audience measurement player) would care a great deal about simultaneously transforming the development model and costs of their increasingly complex technical innovations for audience measurement. And at the same time enriching their information platform way beyond their current goals.

Inhibitors/Consequences?

- Legacy – It's amazing how largely untouched the measurement business has been by the huge shifts in technologies with which to reach and engage consumers, including the mobile applications and cloud-based services implicit in the scenario above. The legacy inhibitors are apparently huge, and the reaction times glacial, both technically, and as a mindset (today's Nielsen initiatives feel like cousins in spirit of cable's enormously complex, legacy-constrained projects from Canoe to Television Everywhere).

- "You can't handle the truth!" – you may recall the uproar over what DVR-measured program (Live + SD) or commercial ratings (C3) *might* reveal. The implicit fear was that someone's emperor would be shown to be unclothed. If these measurements showed massive commercial skipping, this would be to the embarrassment and detriment of players up and down the industry, whether broadcasters, ad agencies, media buyers, and so forth. Even worse, once the toothpaste was out of the tube and this truth was revealed, it could not be hidden and explained away.

But, somewhat surprisingly, while the DVR-based measurements are arguably more accurate, they showed remarkably little commercial skipping, and sometimes re-watching of a show (and its commercials), kind of like free make-goods built in. Hmmm, sounds like "engagement."

In this scenario, though, a political question remains: would an audience measurement company want to discover potentially bad news for its customers?

- Expendable? – Perhaps the worst possible consequence of this scenario is discovering that the Nielsens of the industry aren't even necessary. By handing out an iPod Touch to ten thousand viewers, stocked with a simple app and some data analysis in the back office, couldn't TV networks, or Google, or Amazon do this on their own?

Arguably audience measurement companies like Nielsen today provide more value than just data collection, and would in fact be positioned to provide a great deal *more* analysis, insight, and value in this future scenario than they do today. Also, and this is perhaps the most fundamental point, the television industry is unlikely to walk away from a neutral third-party measurement agent – one of TV's great assets is that unlike the wild west of internet "metrics" and click fraud, ratings generally mean something and can be relied on to reflect actual audience behavior within the margins of error of the measurement process.

The bottom line: a wild card in the long-term convergence of today's TV with the internet is how advertisers will think about, or even help drive/retard that evolution. One view is that among the key forces driving the evolution will be future audience measurement and its relationship to the future of media buying.

In theory, the much-bemoaned fragmentation of the television market should, from an advertisers point of view, be largely irrelevant. If you can't find the reach you need in a few programs and channels, keep buying until you pile up the GRPs (gross ratings points), adjust the frequency, check the demos, and presto your media plan is implemented.

In day-to-day reality, of course, it's far from being that simple. Both because endless details can easily derail the intent of a media plan – the complexity of purchasing through ad networks, checking and rating the inventory, managing the mix, auditing, getting make-goods, etc. – and because the mindset remains that higher-rated programs should command a premium above and beyond the scale they deliver.

In other words, you might be able to piece together a television buy that takes a few mid-rated NBC shows, some cable fare and (almost) equals exposure on *American Idol*, but it's still not the same as what *Idol* delivers. This is reflected in the structural fact (covered in Chapter II, see Exhibit II-6) that to reach an audience of ten million, to buy one 30-second weekday prime-time spot would cost, say, $300,000, vs. reaching two audiences of five million for a total of $240,000. The $60,000 "premium" for ostensibly the same result is from the scarcity value of the single spot, in turn driven by the underlying belief that such a hit show delivers, well, something extra – buzz, engagement, a halo for the advertiser, whatever.

Clearly there's an arbitrage opportunity. More behavior-based, and broad based audience measurement as in the scenario above could have the unintended, yet disruptive effect of commoditizing ad placement. Or not! If Nielsen et al can demonstrate measurable value characteristics beyond reach and demos, then that could allow even more objectively-measurable value premiums and pricing variety based on a richer understanding of viewer behavior and segmentation. That would be awfully close to the long-sought audience measurement Holy Grail.

*   *   *   *   *

Let's turn to the last two of our scenarios that are directed squarely at the matter at hand – what are some endgames that might reflect how Hollywood and its distribution channels resolve the transition from cable-centric to more "open", internet-based program distribution?

Hollywood Everywhere

For this scenario, we're going to take the title (and the reference to strategy in Chapter IV, see Exhibit IV-2) pretty literally – wherever you can plausibly consume media, television is available, and it's Hollywood itself, not distributors, that's large and in charge.

Background: sometime around 2015

- Hulu, now a public company, becomes a bit too independent for its own good, turning on its former owners and acting as an Apple-like gatekeeper of content, deciding who shall pay and who shall play, increasingly monopolizing streaming distribution of commercial television programming

- Rights and windowing deals, while still individually chaotic seeming, collectively become more coherent, with studios innovating new rights classes for internet exhibition and syndication, and winding down broader licensing and carriage agreements as they expire

- In a chance dinner between a number of US Big Media CEOs and Roberto Marinho, CEO of Brazil's Globo television empire, the American executives are astonished to learn what their underlings in the international back office have long known – the vast majority of programming deals in Brazil are entirely mediated by Net Brasil a (Globo-dominated) marketplace/licensing intermediary.

Who's Up/Who's Down?

- *UP:* Hulu – given a huge head start by its original network shareholders (Disney, News Corp., NBCU), Hulu continues to move forward as the integrated, go-to site for most TV programming. Its library depth continues to increase and windowing vs. live/linear TV is incrementally more flexible. Most of the viewing growth is driven by short-form content accessed via mobile devices

- *UP (sort of):* cable systems – despite the tortured implementation of Television Everywhere and Hulu's continued growth, it's pretty much business as usual in the cable world with only slightly increased churn/erosion of the subscriber base.

- *DOWN:* advertisers – major US advertisers are again threatening a rebellion against TV ad rates and internet ad networks, driven by increasing frustration with the "death of a thousand cuts" fragmentation that persists year after year, with no structural remedies to the ad buying inefficiency (and questionable ad effectiveness) yet in sight.

Actions

- Sensing the threat that Hulu is becoming "the next cable monopoly" and that it has become the Frankenstein monster of internet distribution, Hollywood bands together to restructure the entire television distribution marketplace in a sweeping change not seen since the expiration of Fin-Syn (see Chapter I)

- Inspired by the Brazilian example, the major studios create 'NetUSA', an "open and transparent marketplace" (US Department of Justice take note) and clearinghouse for program licensing for *all* delivery channels

- NetUSA throws open the doors to all comers, promptly licensing at Hulu MFN (most-favored nation) rates and terms the equivalent library to Amazon, Pandora, Netflix, Amazon, and Google.

- Mindful of the advertiser unrest, NetUSA creates the "NetOne" advertiser program, supplanting the network upfronts and the juicier slices of the spot market, as well as facilitating "integrated" and near real-time media buys across broadcast and internet formats

- "Independent" cable channels (i.e. not affiliated with Big Media conglomerates such as Time-Warner or Viacom or Disney) clamor to join the NetUSA marketplace under similar terms, while Hulu belatedly offers its own "real-time auction market" in a lame attempt to counter Hollywood's reconsolidation of distribution and advertising sales power.

Inhibitors/Consequences?

- In reality, structural changes of this magnitude require major catalysts, though usually they can only be seen in hindsight. The demise of Fin-Syn, which had prohibited vertical integration of production and syndication, was only part of what unleashed a wave of Big Media consolidation and prosperity. The continuation of Reagan-era deregulation, and easy money for M&A were major contributors to the consolidation and restructuring of the media business.

- The "true" relationship between Hulu and its shareholders remains, externally at least, a mystery. While very much an independent consumer brand, its current CEO strives to position Hulu within the industry as an entrepreneurial "start up." This is certainly politic vis-à-vis Hollywood's relationship with the cable industry. But it may also be symptomatic of a split personality or mixed agenda that could one day turn on its shareholders/suppliers.

The bottom line: driven as much by the annoyance of interminable carriage and retrans battles with cable, and the specter of Hulu dictating internet distribution terms, and the threat of an advertiser buyers' strike, Hollywood decides it's had enough. With Hulu paving the way towards demonstrated viewer value for internet-delivered programming, Hollywood throws open the barn doors, making every credible online outlet a place where its wares can be viewed, rented, or bought, while enabling a consolidated marketplace for suppliers and advertisers.

*   *   *   *   *

Pax Coaxica

In the US at least, telcos will in all likelihood continue to be bit players in the unfolding video distribution drama. While, over time, they will accrete a few single-digit millions of video subscribers, the real action remains in the cable (and satellite) showdown vs. the internet.

Video aside, however, the increasingly-forgotten overall strategic saga of AT&T (and telcos generally) is moderately instructive background for this scenario (the story is recounted in some detail in an old report of ours: "Transformation Interrupted: Can Telecom Be Saved From Itself?", available on the web.)

Briefly, under then-CEO Michael Armstrong, AT&T began a broadband buying binge, purchasing John Malone's TCI in 1998, and then going after US West's former cable roll-up, MediaOne, in 1999. These acquisitions collectively totaled over $80 billion and, along with AT&T's wireless services division were viewed as big, bold plays for the future. How this all worked out is left to the reader to recollect and/or research, but let's just say that in Leslie Cauley's excellent book, *End of the Line: The Rise and Fall of AT&T*, it was revealed how the company came within inches of bankruptcy.

The take-away for our purposes, however, is the propensity of large network players to want to hop from one big technology play to the next, especially when the going gets rough in a "legacy" business. Rather than apply some creative thought to, say, rejuvenating or at least maintaining their historical wireline franchise, telcos have watched it rot, to a large degree needlessly, with each wireline disconnect a wire that will almost certainly never be reconnected and upgraded to provide, oh, broadband or TV. In the US, broadband should have been by all rights a fundamental telco slam dunk, yet the carriers watched as the cable industry levered their own wires to walk away with the lion's share of a brand new and lucrative category of service from a starting point of zero.

In the world of official telco strategy, this is "good." It freed them to focus on the Next Big Thing – wireless – which has indeed become really, really big and to go play yet another half-hearted round of one of their favorite games "Let's Move Up The Value Chain!" in which they fantasize about becoming movie studios or important intermediaries in the music business, or "partners" with Apple, or whatever. In the meantime they protect EBITDA by divesting employees and about-to-implode assets.

The most skilled practitioner of the strategic divestiture has been Verizon, which managed to offload Hawaiian Telephone to private equity investor The Carlyle Group and watch it go bankrupt, offload its directory business (later renamed Idearc) which IPO'd and went bankrupt (upon exiting, renamed SuperMedia, seriously), and offload pesky high-cost rural wireline assets (to FairPoint) and watch those drag their new owner into near-bankruptcy. Game, set, and match to Ivan Seidenberg.

All this prefatory talk about telecom to set up our scenario is simply to (re)familiarize you with an important chapter of a tried and true telecom playbook. In our hypothetical case, cable eagerly borrows a few of its choicest pages.

Background: sometime around 2015

- Hulu and its cousins (Amazon, Netflix, Apple) begin to make substantial inroads into television viewing with 15% (a huge, "tipping point" amount) of HH spent viewing migrating to internet-delivered programming, away from linear, usually cable-provided TV.

- The increasingly "a la carte" internet viewing behavior puts further pressure on the still-languishing cable (now joined by satellite) Television Everywhere initiatives.

- Broadband connectivity (e.g. cable modems) is now a largely mature market and under price pressure from emerging 4G wireless broadband suppliers, both "pure plays" like Clearwire, and LTE services from Verizon Wireless et al

- Upselling cable subscribers to HD, 3D, and other premium tiers of digital cable continues to flounder, in part due to the never-ending structural economic recession in the US which has depressed consumer spending and created deflationary price expectations

Who's Up/Who's Down?

- *UP:* Hulu – unambiguously so, with its cousins at Amazon, Netflix, Apple, and Pandora bringing up the rear.

- *UP:* Content owners, who are beginning to reap a modest amount of advertising benefit (dollars not dimes) from the new, now-substantial digital viewing audiences, as we elaborated at length in Chapter II, and are pressuring Hulu et al to revise their revenue split.

- *UP:* Advertisers who are beginning to see real value from (marginally) more targeted, ads at more "engaged" digital viewers, and are becoming more confident about switching a small portion of the advertising mix away from traditional TV at last, at more than just experimental levels.

- *DOWN:* cable, satellite and, to the extent they are relevant, telco video distribution businesses. A tiny, but very threatening minority of "cord cutting" viewers are finally becoming able to piece together a satisfactory video entertainment mix without using traditional, tiered, multi-channel video providers like cable and satellite

Actions

- Much as major US wireless carriers (e.g. Verizon, AT&T and to a lesser extent Sprint) initially dismissed and ignored flat-rate, all-you-can-eat wireless plans from MetroPCS and Leap as "not a product," cable companies initially dismiss a la carte internet video consumption. But they redouble industry advertising campaigns showing happy families luxuriating in the benefits of "real" television service and bundled savings...everywhere.

- Sensing weakness, a few broadcast networks and cable channels begin ratcheting up carriage and retrans fees during the next round of negotiations with mid-sized cable players, and refusing to grant or renew internet exhibition rights.

- Responding to video service disconnect rates that are becoming eerily reminiscent of telco wireline loss rates five to ten years ago, cable grudgingly promotes cheaper, entry-level video packages at the magic $40-50 per month level, including "up to 2 hours" of online program viewing per month.

- Having only recently finished aggregating and rationalizing their national networks, cable companies begin peeling off unprofitable properties and divesting them to private equity firms

- Comcast/NBC cleans house, divesting a number of marginal channel properties, dropping carriage of 20% of its channels, and beginning substantial workforce reductions

- Comcast launches a take-over offer for Clearwire, touting the synergies with a "next-generation" wireless video-delivery network.

The bottom line: cable has no choice but to streamline, accept more modest circumstances, and adapt its focus to delivery infrastructure. It is forced to give up (most prominently in Comcast/NBC's case) on its hybrid content/distribution strategy to protect a rapidly eroding distribution business, while restructuring its business for diminished market share.

The scenario title – "Pax Coaxica" – implies that after the dust settles, the market does ultimately reach some form of at least interim equilibrium. Imagine such an endgame based on the characteristics we discussed in Chapter IV (in the section, "Hollywood Everywhere: Digital as We Need to Be"), wherein cable companies re-allocate bandwidth away from video and towards higher-speed broadband, re-evaluate programming tiers and price structures, and so forth.

As we discussed in our hypothetical segmentation (Exhibit IV-5), the video market will "convert" gradually and in segments (not necessarily the ones we hypothesized), over an extended period of time. So we can imagine periods of comparative peace in which a day-to-day truce between the Hulus and the Comcasts prevails, until such time as the world turns again and evolves beyond this imaginary scenario.

*   *   *   *   *

Epilog: Why Not?

Movies, TV shows, and books often end with a typical formula. After a long journey, the "real" message is distilled, things come to a close on an inspirationally upbeat note, with perhaps a bit of "you can do it" exhortation thrown in for good measure. Roll credits.

Okay, so let's try going with that.

It was quite a few pages ago that we introduced the distinction (and connection) between what we called television's "macro" or marketplace problem and its "micro" or user experience problem. We asserted that watching TV has become too hard in two respects – an industry-level fragmentation problem making it harder than ever to connect viewers and programs effectively (and economically), and the everyday problem of a confused, frustrated viewer sitting on a couch trying to find what she wants to watch whether on a TV set or a laptop or a phone.

Neither of these problems is going to be solved by the wrong industries innovating in the wrong way.

We've looked at and debunked the multi-decade history (a history repeating itself at this very moment), of cable and telephone companies' grandiose visions of Television of the Future. And we've noted the limitations of Hollywood's own initial efforts. It won't be enough to have a television website, however nicely implemented, whose content weakly and confusingly parallels (sort of) the already-fragmented programming supply that overwhelms today's viewers. And the more of these websites there are, the more we're back to square one as they will contribute to, not remedy, the very fragmentation they aim to stem.

Someone, it could be Hollywood (it *should* be Hollywood), is going to crack the problem of letting viewers get what they want. Of engineering the capabilities for a simple "personal program guide" which completely changes how viewers interact with sources of TV programs, in a way that DVRs only marginally managed to help. Of insulating viewers from not only the still-increasing frustration of fragmented program supply, but from the complexities of consuming media across so many different platforms or devices. Of treating television as an application.

Whoever does that is going to have the power to reshape and profit from the rebuilt relationship between viewer and content provider, silencing a lot of the abstract yammering about "social media," "brand conversations," "engagement," and "digital dimes." The talk will be supplanted with concrete, easy-to-use functionality that becomes part of consumers daily lives, because television is part of consumers daily lives.

Hollywood's initial response to the internet "threat" has been rational, well-implemented, and effective. But the game is rapidly getting more complicated. Too many players from too many industries with too many agendas are encroaching too quickly on too many fronts – game console makers, Apple, Google, even cable companies themselves.

A smooth-talking Netflix or an Amazon can't wait for the day when Hollywood wakes up to find it has inadvertently made these retailers into a combined new Wal-Mart and next-generation cable system. Imagine complete domination of electronic TV distribution in ways that would make Wal-Mart's buying leverage and historical share of the DVD sell-through market look paltry by comparison.

Does Hollywood have what it takes to connect directly to its viewers and shape the next media business models in its favor? At what scale can this be done? Send your bosses off to the next Sun Valley conference with phrases like "television is an application" and "personal program guide," and "not Television Everywhere, but Hollywood Everywhere!" while back home you work on getting the television industry ready for its next sixty years. Why not?

Appendix

Hollywood Opts Out of the Google Economy
December 2005

Hollywood has rationally calculated that, for some time to come, large-scale broadband video distribution would only destroy proven value, fail to provide alternative value, and alter a business model that is still far from being in decline. With near-total control of the most valuable program libraries and the business models governing their distribution, a shift towards broadband media will come largely on Hollywood's terms and at an incremental pace.

Barbarians at the Gate: Fears of a "Google-like" disruption of film and television are misplaced

Google Bad

Wall Street Journal columnist Alan Murray succinctly summarized the media industry's resentment of Google's business model: "The Google economy is a kind of high-tech feudal system: The peasants produce the content; Google makes the profits."[1]

1   GoogleLibrary Is Great for the World, *The Wall Street Journal*, October 26, 2005

Another journalist framed media's unease in the context of recent dotcom history: "...the internet is back...its potential for radical disruption is [now] married to the capacity for outlandish profits. Once again, the media village senses that the wolf is at the door. But the village suspects that this time, he's not going away, and that he's brought some friends. The village has been wrong before. But probably not now."[2]

Google, as well as Yahoo! (Nasdaq: YHOO) and Microsoft's (Nasdaq: MSFT) MSN, have been adept at creating value (principally advertising revenue) by re-packaging and re-presenting the content of others in search- and community-driven contexts. Having reinvented the advertising business and shifted substantial ad spending its way, Google is intent on rendering books digitally accessible (as is Microsoft), providing municipal wireless broadband, venturing into online classifieds, and has even made ominous-sounding, if fanciful, conjectures about its potential role in the television advertising market.

Combine fear and uncertainty with blogger gossip about Google job postings or secret fiber optic purchases, mix with speculation about Yahoo's media operations in Santa Monica, add broadcaster announcements about prime-time iPod downloads, and voilà: a "trend" – broadband disruption at the front gate of media's major citadel, with Hollywood itself cast in the role of Sunset Boulevard's ageing Norma Desmond.

Broadband Interference
The generalized fear of broadband and its power to disrupt existing business models is far from unfounded. Futurists apply it to television roughly as follows – with more broadband-connected households than ever, programming will be made available in increasingly massive video-on-demand libraries accessed over the internet, wired or wireless, fixed or mobile.

---

2   Googlephobia, *New York Magazine*, December 5, 2005, John Heilemann

Like newspapers being electronically disaggregated into individual stories accessed over the web, video content will be atomized into individual programs for personalized consumption. The concept of a "channel" or broadcast day parts like "prime time", as well as even the need for traditional distribution networks like station groups, or cable and satellite systems will disappear. And an atomized, broadband-delivered video world will lead to all manner of new forms of 'interactive' media supplanting today's entertainment.

Recent news flow might lead one to believe that US television networks are either: (a) boldly experimenting with broadband media, (b) starting to panic about the internet, (c) slow-moving dinosaurs resisting broadband at every turn, or (d) seeing the coming broadband threats are about to unwind their generally coöperative relationship with cable and satellite operators in favor of an "every man for himself" distribution strategy.

We believe the answer for now is: (e) none of the above.

In past weeks there have been a series of broadband-sounding announcements from Viacom's (NYSE: VIA) CBS, GE's (NYSE: GE) NBC Universal, and Disney's (NYSE: DIS) ABC publicizing various forms of new programming delivery, including to video iPods.

These offers are, deliberately, about as narrow and as far as one could get from a media disruption, despite some of the accompanying saber-rattling, carriage-fee-requiring remarks about "cable bypass" from Viacom co-president and head of CBS, Leslie Moonves.

A very limited slate of prime-time shows (not coincidentally, ones produced by the networks' captive studios) are made available in a Video on Demand (VoD) format through existing distribution channels (cable, satellite), though ABC and NBC are offering $1.99 "vidcasts" to video iPods. In the case of cable-bypassing CBS, the VoD shows are to be distributed via Comcast (Nasdaq: CMCSA), the US' largest cable operator, and only in markets with CBS O&Os, and only in a one-week window after initial over-the-air exhibition.

These limited, 'non-linear' forms of prime-time program delivery signal that broadcast networks, far from capitulating to a "trend", intend to fully protect any incremental viewing rights enabled by new technologies (VoD or otherwise). The message to distributors – cable, satellite, or anyone else: "New technology-enabled monetization of our programming will be under our control, with our consent."

No one, including US broadcast networks, would disagree that video content is well suited to broadband distribution. And we can expect to see accelerating innovations in both broadband-tailored content and distribution models. But dreams (or fears) of a "Google-like", rapid upending of the television and film industry are misplaced.

What Hollywood really believes was summarized best and most directly by Peter Chernin, News Corporation's (NYSE: NWS) President and Chief Operating Officer in their last quarterly earnings call. Speaking of Fox Television's notable absence from the recent flurry of announcements, he observed: "the last thing we're worried about is [that] we're going to somehow miss opportunities here...we're talking about establishing precedents for some time to come..."

We believe change will come largely on Hollywood's terms and at an incremental pace, for reasons we outline and quantify below. Before doing so, one caveat or disclaimer. As with the history of telecom innovation, it is very likely that broadband media's first high-performance examples of both business models and technology deployments will be provided outside the US.

In particular, we have in mind the UK television market which already has a mix of: high levels of TV viewing, forceful public policy, lower dependence on advertising, very high degrees of digital video penetration (including digital terrestrial service), and early adoption of interactive services, among other factors.

2006 promises to make the UK the much-watched bellwether market. Among the milestone events, the BBC is expected to move aggressively towards broadband content distribution, and BT Group (NYSE ADS: BT) is expected to enter the video services market with what promises to be a significantly differentiated television offer, unlike its US telco counterparts.

For better or worse, Hollywood dominates the global filmed entertainment business. And in markets where American products are in the minority there is almost always media concentration, and hence library control, comparable to or greater than that found in the US. This occurs via quasi-governmental entities, media oligopolies, or both. But there are also substantial local variations in media business models, and so our opinions and analysis below have only the US media market in mind.■

Rational Hollywood: Broadband is cast in a supporting role for now

Show Me The Money

The vast majority of desirable mass market video content and the business model for its distribution are still firmly under Hollywood's control. While residential broadband penetration continues to grow, other important catalysts for a shift towards broadband media consumption, from new syndication windows, to broadband-connected televisions or their set-top boxes, to suitable home networking technology, are still on the horizon.

Hollywood can afford to plant a few seeds, monitor fledgling competitors, weigh in on still-emerging delivery technologies, but wait for broadband media opportunities to become more clearly big enough and profitable enough to warrant serious mind-share or capital.

In the meantime, Hollywood's agenda is to realize further gains from vertical integration and use broadband in a supporting role. Broadband technology is used to reduce marketing costs and reinforce viewer involvement with existing products (enhancing advertising and syndication value). Over time, Hollywood will reassess broadband opportunity in light of three major barriers— production and distribution economics, and market size and evolution:

(1) Production – broadband is far from economically viable

US television studios almost always lose money on their expensively-created content until it is resold after initial broadcast network licensing. DVD sales account for an increasing, if still small, proportion of incremental revenues and this window is likely to be the first to transition to lower-cost broadband distribution.

But the real turning point in television series profitability occurs with off-net syndication. This resale occurs in relatively large program blocks, often 110 episodes or five seasons worth, enabling "stripped" syndication in which programs are re-exhibited in the same time slot five days a week.

These off-net syndication rights, which don't allow for broadband distribution, have often been locked up for years to come. And given the wholesale nature of the business, it is not unusual to license practically the full slate of a studio's output for a multi-year period. A broadband carve-out for newly-available syndication rights is certainly possible, but with fees running well above $100 million for a hit one-hour drama, the existing syndication model sets an enormously high bar for replacement or separately-negotiated incremental revenues from broadband rights.

Series Economics (1-Hour Drama)

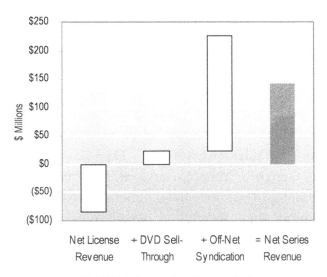

Exhibit A-1 – Series Economics)

"If you want to get added to the windowing scheme, you have to pay your way in …There's no benefit to any of us doing business with those guys [i.e. Google et al] on a micro-transactional basis."

— Anonymous network executive.

Prime-time TV fare will not join the Google Economy because, for some time to come, widespread broadband distribution would only destroy proven value, fail to provide alternative value, and alter a business model that is still far from declining. As one network distribution executive said recently, "If you want to get added to the windowing scheme, you have to pay your way in …There's no benefit to any of us doing business with those guys [i.e. Google et al] on a micro-transactional basis."

Hypothetically, say Google or Yahoo! did "pay their way in" to create a broadband window. Rather than tackle the issue of a parallel window and how much it must pay to compensate for discounting the value of traditional off-net syndication, let us assume a straight-up replacement in order to shed light on the economics.

Aspiring to marquee fare, our hypothetical broadband media buyers are bidding for the domestic syndication rights for the police drama "Law & Order." To successfully compete against cable channels, they might pay on the order of $150 million.

Having taken the show off the cable market and put it instead into broadband distribution (and hence a more 'internet-like' business model), they might treat that expense, at least conceptually, as part of traffic acquisition costs (TAC). Then, to match their current profitability Google or Yahoo! would have to find a way to deploy this video content (just one show, remember) to generate around $350M in advertising, subscription, or some other kind of revenues, well over a $100 million more than comparable cable syndication would be likely to generate.

In the US, significant broadband distribution of top shelf television fare is, to put it mildly, highly unlikely any time soon. What's on the line is not just the syndication revenues themselves, but an entire business system for which broadband distribution is, as yet, unable to provide a compelling alternative or even complementary path forward.

But cheaper, independently-created or older content, less constrained by complex syndication and rights structures will gradually find its way to broadband, with still unknown demand or results. This is already happening via Time-Warner's (NYSE: TWX) AOL unit and their planned 'In2TV' broadband offer, as well as early content agreements with entrepreneurial broadband video distributors such as Akimbo, Brightcove, and Maven Networks.

(2) Distribution – broadband plays a supporting role
Beginning in the early '90s, the US television market has been increasingly deregulated and, partially as a consequence, more vertically integrated. With the disappearance of regulatory

restrictions, most notably 'Fin-Syn'[3], media companies have integrated their production and broadcast businesses, created new forms of distribution (DVD sell-through, captive cable channels), and managed advertising sales and program windowing to optimize returns across this integrated portfolio.

As exploitation of integration synergies continues and entertainment-related business models further converge, distinctions between "broadcast" and "cable", for example, become less meaningful[4]. The much publicized decline in broadcast network ad sales in the "upfront" (i.e. forward) market – which accounts for over 80% of inventory – means a lot less when NBC Universal, for example, in addition to studio assets owns or controls Bravo, Telemundo, mun2TV, USA, SciFi, MSNBC, and CNBC.

Controlling cable channels is an industry-wide strategic response of diversifying away from network television's gradual, secular decline and squeezing further scope and scale economies across production and broader range of programming outlets. And Tier 1 cable operators, most notably Comcast, are pursuing similar strategies of diversifying across content ownership, programming outlets, advertising, as well as their infrastructure businesses of video distribution, high-speed internet access and telephony. (CAPTION AND PLACEHOLDER: Exhibit A-2 – Share of US Upfront Market)

The work of expanding such a portfolio and optimizing its revenue yield still has a good deal of remaining upside and strategic work ahead of it. This form of 'convergence', not the technical/broadband kind, is the front line of television competition.

The sharpening of audience measurement technologies,

---

3   Financial Interest and Syndication rules expired in the early '90s, unleashing a major shift in the economics of filmed and television entertainment, starting with consolidation of TV production. Fin-Syn had previously restricted broadcast networks from having a financial interest in programs beyond first-run exhibition, and prohibited the creation of domestic syndication arms.

4   At this point, it is hard to tell what effect Carl Icahn's on-going "break up the company" campaign will have on one of the integrated giants, Time-Warner. Viacom's proposed split, while largely separating broadcast and cable assets appears to be geared at preserving CBS' production economies.

the packaging of media buys around more clearly measurable demographics and focused channel mix, the arrival of ad tagging and insertion systems, the more efficient aggregation of fragmented advertising inventory in regional interconnect systems, and the value-added services potential of digital terrestrial television – all of these provide a full agenda with plenty of profit-enhancing opportunities before addressing broadband as a mainstream delivery medium.

For now, broadband media has a well-defined and growing role in Hollywood, and it is to play a supporting role in the business model convergence agenda, not the other way round. Broadband creates additional ways to involve, sustain and build viewership, thus increasing the value of the core products themselves, including broadcast advertising. For example, a broadcaster may wish to:

- *further monetize proven viewer demographics* by adding an interactive component to a targeted media buy (above average CPMs for, say, visits and/or click-throughs at Fox's 'American Idol' website)

- *sustain broadcast advertising value* by using web-based presence to draw in additional viewers or further involve existing ones ('American Idol' voting, discussion groups)

- *reinforce and build additional value for future monetization* (DVD sell-through and/or program syndication) of captive studio programs by increasing viewer involvement through web-based and mobile interaction (Fox's '24', for example)

Reflected in, for example, recent News Corp. internet-related acquisitions, the effect of Google's success has been to sharpen interest in adding another portfolio element – internet presence and advertising as a complement to, not as a disruptive replacement for Hollywood's core business.

(3) *Market Evolution – a niche for some time to come*

The final and perhaps most limiting characteristic of broadband media as a mainstream opportunity is that it is too small, and is unlikely to compare favorably even to television's existing niche audience outlets for quite some time. The combined effects of special-interest channels (e.g. Food Network), conventionally-delivered on-demand programming (e.g. cable or satellite VoD), and DVRs (channel disaggregation, time shifting) leave comparatively little room for separately-sourced programs which happen to be delivered as IP packets over broadband connections.

Our view of broadband media's addressable market is that is must account for three factors:

- *adequate bandwidth*

- *propensity to consume broadband media*

- *network-attached televisions*

First, bandwidth. Despite generous growth in at least downstream bandwidth, principally led by cable's high-speed internet services, we believe it is likely that the US median bandwidth per broadband household will stay flat, or even decline. This is because as the market matures, new subscriber additions are principally at the "value" end of the broadband offers.

While offers with headline speeds in the tens or even hundreds of megabits are also likely, consumer need for this level of performance is very limited in the medium term. As broadband connectivity continues to be commoditized, performance levels will be tiered, and consumers will purchase according to price/performance requirements. Some time in the future, it is likely that broadband media may become the application which drives upgrades of broadband connectivity.

In the meantime, roughly 60% of today's broadband households have 'adequate' bandwidth (say, 3Mbps downstream as the minimum) for imagined broadband media offers, with this percentage possibly declining to below 50% in the next five years or so, as broadband penetration into late-adopting households continues. Then, as broadband media becomes a known, desired consumer service, and as DSL (the main source of low-end broadband connectivity) improves, median household bandwidth will turn upward again.

Second, propensity to consume broadband media. Since this market doesn't exist, this is basically anyone's guess, but as with any new product category, the idea that more than say, 30% of potential qualified consumers will adopt it in less than five years, is quite extreme. So let us posit a generous starting point of 20% of broadband households with adequate bandwidth will consume broadband media, and let it grow upward from there.

Third, 'network-attached' televisions. This is a proxy for being able to watch broadband media, sourced independently from "walled garden" cable or satellite content (even if via those operators' set-top boxes), on an actual television in your living room, not on a computer or handheld device. There are certainly a large number of technical enablers on their way, beyond today's awkward offers such as Microsoft's Media Center, adding an independent "broadband antenna" to the living room TV. TiVo's recent announcements of broadband content delivery are a small step in that direction, for example, and this capability is the very definition of entrepreneurial broadband television services such as Akimbo.

But for the near- to medium-term, cable or satellite set-tops will dominate the "last inch" of connecting televisions to digital content. Given the fledgling and awkward state of video-enabling home networking technology, we would doubt that even 5% of today's qualified broadband households have what it takes to directly display network-delivered broadband media on their primary televisions.

Even with what we believe to be generous assumptions, applying these three limitations to define an addressable broadband media market results in some pretty small numbers. By comparison, the

US' largest cable operator (Comcast) and largest direct broadcast satellite service (DirecTV – NYSE: DTV) together have in excess of 35 million subscribers.

Broadband Media Households

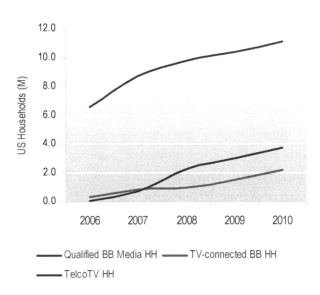

As a point of reference, we also display estimated US Telco TV subscribers – that is, households subscribing to the new generation of phone company television services, not their satellite resale offer. With slight discounting to AT&T (NYSE: T) and Verizon's (NYSE: VZ) announced expectations (since they have already slipped), we assume these offers demonstrate some market success in 2008, leading to additional investment and growing to around 25 million homes passed and 15% penetration by 2010. This penetration level is representative of any third-player undifferentiated offer, and is a typical market share for overbuilders in existing cable markets.

If Telco TV is in fact able to match or exceed the number of network-connected television broadband households, this gives US phone companies a very significant and potentially disruptive opportunity to move to a next-phase differentiated video offer, transforming a me-too offer into one of the leading edges of the broadband media insurgency. We will return to discuss this point a bit later.■

A Confounding Revolution: How we will know it is coming and how to keep score

Interactive Headache

Interviewed several months ago by, of all people, long-time friend and nemesis Michael Eisner, IAC/InterActiveCorp (Nasdaq: IACI) CEO Barry Diller described the complexity of the broadband media challenge this way: "In this interactive, internet world, I mean, you have a headache twenty minutes into the day… Films and television, [are] not a business that, so to speak, confounds you – you're telling stories. But this is. …we're in a revolution, we're absolutely in a radical revolution."

The seeds of a broadband media revolution are already being sown by entrepreneurs unknown and well-known. We have shown why neither Hollywood nor its cable and satellite distribution networks are likely to spark or give much early encouragement to that revolution. Not surprisingly, they have well-functioning business models with much at stake when the revolution takes hold. So where might change come from, and how is it likely to proceed?

Early video wins are likely to share two characteristics: they will check as many boxes as possible in our 'NewTV' wish list below and, through experimentation, successfully match niche audiences or communities with types of programming, just as television does today.

NewTV Wish List	
Incremental revenue	Subscription revenue, advertising, incremental "brand value", etc.
Contextual sponsorship	New basis for advertising or other contextual sponsorship of content presentation
Low/no cannibalization	Distinct category of content consumption which does not cannibalize legacy revenues or content rights
Optimized viewing	Delivered via quality- and performance-assured network services
Content protection	Content rights-holders adequately protected while balancing consumer convenience
TV endpoint	Can be easily viewed on a television directly connected to the service
Breakout HH reach	Drives reach to and past the 50M HH level
Exclusivity (medium-specific)	Sufficiently exclusive (for the chosen delivery medium) to be valuable and uniquely create traffic?

Category	Suitability/Example
Current season prime time mass audience	Limited; very narrow rights window, value vs. DVR questionable
Current (1-5 year old) prime time library	Limited; conflicts with syndication and DVD sell-through, BB unable to deliver replacement revenues, value vs. DVR questionable
Special interest channel	e.g. Hallmark Channel, family; History Channel, hard-to-reach male demos
BB-friendly premium demographics	e.g. 'The Simpsons' (top 40 share, top 10 CPMs), MTV Overdrive, Comedy Channel broadband sampler
"We Media"	e.g. Current TV, Link TV; BB-friendly demos, "interactive", mainstream distribution often out of reach

Exhibit 4 – NewTV Wish List)

Let's imagine you are pitching a new, surefire approach to broadband media distribution – you just need something to distribute and are far from having the resources of, say a Mark Cuban, to build both an independent production company and an independent programming and movie distributor.

To put it more bluntly, you will have to redistribute content developed for television until such time as you can develop your own, or a broadband content renaissance arrives. Your value proposition to consumers is about immediacy, convenience, choice, and price, not cool new shows unavailable elsewhere.

A bit more disappointing news – despite wanting to break out of traditional media concepts you will probably have to package what you offer in something very analogous to a "channel" in today's television world. This is because (a) without some thematic organization and brand, you will (like ineffective web sites in today's internet) simply disappear into the noise, and (b) you will very likely need a fixed subscription fee as part of your revenue model for you to stand a chance of becoming economically viable.

So, you will go to library owners and pitch your business plan, at minimum convincing them that by renting their programs to you their net revenues will be higher by adding you as a distributor than not (see "Incremental Revenue", "Low/No Cannibalization") and that their content will be protected from theft (see "Content Protection").

If your entrepreneurial venture plans to rely on ad revenue, you will need to persuade both library owners and potential advertisers that your financial projections are based on targeted, demographically-valuable reach (see "Contextual Sponsorship", "Exclusivity"), perhaps even with the potential for national scale comparable to traditional media (see "Breakout HH reach"). Finally, for certain classes of content (independent films, for example), you may need to demonstrate your distribution method appropriately showcases, or at least does not degrade, the viewing experience (see "Optimized Viewing", "TV Endpoint").

As to which libraries and types of programming, we've ruled out more than token access to marquee programming at any stage of the syndication pipeline. This leaves three broad approaches, lifted from today's television world, which can be used individually or in combination to match potential audiences and programs:

- *special-interest based*: aggregate a collection of themed programming, often low-cost material that has already run through cable channel syndication and/or is independently marketed

- *demographically-defined:* reverse engineer a possibly eclectic programming line-up from a set of desirable demographics with a high propensity towards broadband usage but low involvement with traditional television (the pitch meeting might go: "it's G4 meets SpikeTV, with a FoxNews sensibility")

- *'We Media':* roughly, a video equivalent of blogging in which audience involvement and viewer-created content ("VC2", as it is known on the recently-launched

'Current TV' channel) creates both an interactive feel and low-programming costs. This two-way characteristic, for which broadband innovation is ideally suited, is either used as an enhancing differentiator or becomes a central, defining element of the programming.

Keeping Score

Barry Diller is probably right that "we're absolutely in a radical revolution", if for no other reason than he is Barry Diller. But how can media, internet, or telecom company strategists separate competitively-important news from noise, and what should investors look for in determining future company prospects?

The list will always change, and probably the most significant events are entirely unforeseen. But the scorecard should focus on anticipating and identifying events signaling meaningful economic developments. Some examples:

Have major independent program developers (e.g. Crown Media, Playboy Enterprises, etc.) made significant library syndication commitments in a broadband-related format? What is the depth of the library under license? How does this deal complement or compete with "linear" exhibition?

- Is Big Media adding significant depth to broadband-available libraries, on what terms, for what distributors, across the board or by genre?

- Are ads or interstitials being inserted in broadband content? Who are the advertisers? Are these barter, in-kind promotional, or cash deals? What audience measurement and reporting, if any, is being employed?

- Is licensed or syndicated broadband-media delivery being linked to a paid-search or internet community model, and if so, how?

- Is anyone developing new broadband-specific content supply (either by re-purposing, similar to wireless carrier 'mobisodes', or with net new production)? What are the reported production costs, who is financing them and how (brand sponsorship, product placement, etc.)?

- Is there any evidence of broadband-related restructuring of rights and windows in lower-profile (cancelled series, cable channel originals, etc.) syndication deals?

- Is there any adoption of "programmer neutral", open devices which can conveniently display broadband content directly on televisions (e.g. TiVo Series2, etc.)?

- Is one of broadband media's potential advantages – à la carte consumption - being eroded by the rise of less-tiered and/or lower-priced subscription services from cable or satellite?

- How are broadcast networks planning on using ancillary spectrum at their O&Os once digital terrestrial television is launched?

Afterword: TelcoTV

Earlier, in discussing the potential size of an independent broadband media market (*Exhibit 3 – Broadband Media Households*) we made passing reference to Telco TV's potential leg up and said we would return to that topic later.

US telcos have four fundamental problems with their TV offers:

- *undifferentiated clones of satellite service* (i.e. "bargain" cable)

- *uneconomic based on programming costs alone*

- *no access to advertising revenues* (no subscribers = no audience to sell) at the very moment in the industry when cable operators are booking double-digit advertising growth and ad insertion technology has the potential to raise CPMs by 50-100%.

- *timing* – drivers of price competition are likely to increase, just as (and partially in consequence of) Telco TV comes to market: e.g. emergence of "value" tiers or quasi-à la carte channel line-ups, no-frills competitors, digital terrestrial service

But telcos also have two valuable advantages: First, a direct path for broadband content to the living room television, not through "Windows Media Centers" or a "Slingbox" or other marginal attachment methods. Second, with no subscribers and high programming costs, telcos do not share cable and satellite's vested interest in "going along" with the Hollywood business model.

The checklist (*Exhibit 4 – NewTV Wish List*) and scorecard immediately above are, among other things, a partial framework for how US telcos might differentiate their me-too video offers at comparatively low incremental cost and establish a modicum of market power in the programming supply chain. Instead of focusing on yesterday's definition of multi-channel television service, a stripped-down offer, supplemented by broadband-enabled library innovation may be Telco's best long-term bet for a sustainable video business.|

Related Reading from i2 Partners

Our "War of the Worlds" reports assess the strategic future of broadband competition. You can Google the following items which provide additional insights on media-related strategies:

- *War of the Worlds: Who Gets Broadband's Profits?* 2005

- *"Viewer's Choice": Entertainment and Telco Transformation* – a hypothetical scenario for broadband video competition in the year 2010

Suggested Reading

Brandenberger, Adam M. and Nalebuff, Barry J. *Co-Opetition* New York: Doubleday Business, 1996 (First Edition)

Cauley, Leslie. *End of the Line: The Rise and Fall of AT&T* New York: Free Press, 2005

Center for Research Excellence. *Video Consumer Mapping Study: Key Findings Report* New York: CRE, 2009

Edgerton, Gary R. *The Columbia History of American Television*. New York: Columbia University Press, 2007

Gitlin, Todd *Inside Prime Time*. New York: Random House, 1983

Gould, Lewis L. *Watching Television Come of Age: The New York Times Reviews by Jack Gould* . Austin: University of Texas Press, 2002

Hoffman, Bob *The Ad Contrarian: Getting Beyond the Fleeting Trends, False Goals, and Dreadful Jargon of Contemporary Advertising*. San Francisco: Hoffman | Lewis, 2009

Jenkins, Henry *Convergence Culture: Where Old and New Media Collide*. New York: New York University Press, 2006

Krug, Steve *Don't Make Me Think: A Common Sense Approach to Web Usability*. Berkeley: New Riders Publishing, 2006 (Second Edition)

Weaver, Pat and Thomas M. Coffey_*The Best Seat in the House: The Golden Years of Radio and Television*. New York: Knopf, 1994

Carr, Nicholas "Is Google Making Us Stupid?" *The Atlantic Monthly*, July/August 2008: 56+ Print.

56+ Print.

Gould, Jack "The Paradoxical State of Television." *New York Times Magazine*, 30 March 1947. 14. Print.

"Idea Man." *Newsweek*, 7 April 1952: 60. Print.

"NBC Presidents Exit Smiling." *Fortune* Summer 1953: 48-49. Print.

"Profile: S.L. Weaver." *The New Yorker* 16 October 1954: 37-38. Print.

"End of the Weaver Era at NBC." *Business Week* 15 September1956: 32. Print.

Index

www.ingramcontent.com/pod-product-compliance
Lightning Source LLC
LaVergne TN
LVHW042137040326
832903LV00011B/285/J